Praise for *Superpod*

"*Superpod* is a collection of incredible ways scientists and activists are exploring the biology, behavior, and plight of Southern Resident orcas. Perfect for readers curious about a career in marine biology or conservation, there are passages that put the reader face-to-face with the whales of the Salish Sea as the author writes about her own experiences in the field. By incorporating the work of other scientists and activists, Nickum's text will expand the reader's understanding of what it means to study whales, the new tools that are in use, and how many questions we still have left to answer."

—**Lindsay Moore**, author of *Yoshi and the Ocean*

"A riveting read! Every sentence shimmers with the author's love and concern for these magnificent animals. Nora Nickum presents the challenges these magnificent animals face with unflinching honesty, yet her message is ultimately uplifting and hopeful. The book encourages and empowers kids to become community scientists, and to be part of the solution to save the orcas."

—**Sarah Albee**, author of *Accidental Archaeologists*

"*Superpod* tells the incredible story of our endangered Southern Resident killer whales and will raise awareness and inspire stewardship in the next generation of orca advocates. Nora Nickum weaves together cutting-edge scientific results and the emotional connection we have with orcas in a compelling and relatable way, bringing a new audience to the table. The science and compassion throughout *Superpod* are both essential to understanding the threats the Southern Residents face and influencing the actions everyone, including young readers, can take to support recovery now and into the future."

—**Lynne Barre**, NOAA recovery coordinator
for Southern Resident killer whales

"You will love diving into the watery world of the orcas! . . . Meet orca individuals and their families and learn how they 'talk' to each other, hunt, play, and try to survive in a place they've called home for thousands of years. What you'll find is that these super-smart creatures are a lot like us in so many ways! Fascinating!"

—**Chris Morgan**, ecologist, filmmaker,
and host of *THE WILD with Chris Morgan*

"*Superpod* delivers a compelling narrative. . . . The book highlights similarities between people and whales, not only as individuals who play, teach, and grieve, but as social 'superpods' that can work together across generations for positive change. Thoughtful discussions of difficult subjects like orcas in captivity and thorough explanations of the science and technology used to study whales will engage and educate readers of all ages."

—**Dr. Danna Staaf**, marine biologist
and author of *The Lady and the Octopus*

SUPERPOD

Saving the Endangered Orcas of the Pacific Northwest

Nora Nickum

Copyright © 2023 by Nora Nickum
Published by Chicago Review Press Incorporated
814 North Franklin Street
Chicago, Illinois 60610
ISBN 978-1-64160-793-3

Library of Congress Control Number: 2022951412

Interior design: Sarah Olson
Map design: Chris Erichsen Cartography

Printed in the United States of America
5 4 3

For Sabina, Amelia, and Hazel, who are already
speaking up for endangered animals like the orcas.

~~~~~~~

The story of orcas and salmon is intertwined with that
of the Coast Salish people, and this book was written
on their traditional and contemporary territories. I
acknowledge and am grateful for their stewardship
of these lands and waters since time immemorial.

Contents

Introduction ～ 1

1 Tahlequah: 17 Days and 1,000 Miles ～ 9

2 What's in a Name? ～ 15

3 The Daily Special ～ 21

4 Conversations Beneath the Waves ～ 29

5 The Bonds of Family ～ 39

6 Dark History ～ 47

7 From the Air ～ 63

8 Whale Doctors ～ 73

9 Mystery of the Breach ～ 83

10 Where Giants Can Still Disappear ～ 93

11 Why Are Other Orcas
Doing Better? ~ 103

12 The Canine in the Superpod ~ 109

13 Finding Friends ~ 123

14 An Ocean Full of Noise ~ 129

15 Quieting the Waters ~ 143

16 When Salmon Return ~ 153

*Epilogue: The Hope in a Superpod,
     and an Invitation* ~ 163

Acknowledgments ~ 171

J Pod Family Tree ~ 173

Maps ~ 176

Resources for Readers and Teachers ~ 178

Notes ~ 181

Index ~ 186

Introduction

The rising sun illuminates a puff of mist, and a black fin slips above the waves. The unmistakable sound of the air from the orca's blowhole—*pfewww*—reaches me a moment later. One after another, or sometimes at the same time, more orcas surface. They exhale and inhale, the soft rhythm occasionally punctuated by a tail slap.

I'm with my friends, all of us high schoolers, on San Juan Island in northern Washington State. It's an island covered with fir forests, pebbly beaches, and twisty madrone trees with peeling red bark. Our sleeping bags lie in dew-laden grass near the rocky cliffs that line the Salish Sea.

Pfewww. There it is again. It's a sound I would know anywhere, one that always makes my heart skip a beat. A sound that wakes me up as well as any alarm.

We watch as the black fins rise and fall. One orca is a youngster who comes up for air in a quick, curvy motion I imagine to be a playful frolic. Others are moms, aunts, brothers, or sisters. There's an adult male, the dorsal fin on his back reaching higher than the rest.

In 20 minutes the orcas are gone, hidden by the next point of land. I let out a deep breath myself. I'm already longing for their next visit. Maybe I'll be lucky and see them again before we leave the island, or maybe I'll have to wait until I return next summer and resume my vigil.

Orcas, about 50,000 in all, are everywhere from tropical waters to the icy seas of Antarctica. But they're not all the same. Groups of orcas have unique cultures, eat different things, and make different calls.

The orcas that awakened me from that high-school campout were from one of those distinct populations, known as the Southern Residents. Their range includes the inland waters of the Pacific Northwest, where I saw them, but also the coastal waters from southeast Alaska to California. Swimming past places where many people live, they let us get to know them. They're a tight-knit family—playful, smart, and caring. And they've captured people's hearts, including my own, in a special

A Southern Resident orca breaches out of the water. *Jill Hein*

way. People have given them names like Blackberry, Tahlequah, Cookie, Eclipse, Kiki, and Phoenix. When one is born, or one dies, it makes the national news, and people celebrate or grieve.

The Southern Residents survived a terrible decade when family members were caught and sent to marine parks. Today, living in noisy, dirty waters without enough food, they're in danger again.

These are the orcas I want you to meet if you haven't already. They've been studied more than any other orca population, yet still manage to fascinate and puzzle us. They are remarkable animals—and they need our help.

~~~~~

The Southern Residents look for food separately, in three small groups called J, K, and L pods, but sometimes they all come together in one place. Imagine people at a fun-filled family reunion, with food and games and hugging and catching up. It's like that—but underwater. This joyous orca gathering, filled with tail- and fin-slaps, is known as a superpod.

Years ago, people observed superpod events from San Juan Island several times each summer, but now these

A Killer Reputation

Orcas are also known as killer whales, perhaps because centuries ago, fishermen and whalers saw them killing other whales. And indeed, orcas are the top predators in the ocean and have been for some 10 million years. But there's no record of a wild orca ever killing a human. The term "orca" comes from their scientific name, *Orcinus orca*. It may stir more empathy for these amazing and struggling creatures, even though some say the Latin name roughly translates as "demon from hell"! But really, orcas have only had one enemy: people.

events are rare—seen perhaps once a year, or less. The Southern Residents seldom find enough food in one spot to enjoy a collective feast.

My job is to help these orcas. As a policy advocate for the Seattle Aquarium, I make sure our laws protect the orcas and the ocean. The Southern Resident orcas need a healthier environment to overcome the very real risk of going extinct within your lifetime. As predators at the top of the food chain, their plight is also a big warning signal. If they're in trouble, the whole ecosystem is in trouble.

When I was on that campout with my friends, over two decades ago, there were 89 Southern Resident orcas. But the number was beginning to drop.

In fall 2020, I return to San Juan Island, as I have every summer since I was five years old. I time my visits for

Can you spot the fourth orca? *Danielle Carter*

Three Pods, One Family

The Southern Resident pods are named J, K, and L because their distant relatives up in Canada, known as the Northern Residents, got the earlier part of the alphabet. L pod is the largest of the three Southern Resident pods, and K pod is the smallest. J pod, the medium-sized one, has traditionally spent the most time in the busy waters of the Salish Sea, giving us extra opportunities to get to know them. Together, the three Southern Resident pods are called a clan. It's one big extended family.

the months when Southern Resident orcas have historically been seen here most often. But now, there are only 73 remaining, and the government has declared them critically endangered.

The prior summer, I hadn't spotted a single Southern Resident orca. So I've gone two years without seeing one, and I miss them like I would miss seeing my family. But I'm still tuned in to the frequency of their breaths, just in case.

One evening at dusk, I'm collecting the remnants of dinner from the picnic table when suddenly I hear it. *Pfewww.* I run down to the sea, and there they are. Far out, perhaps a dozen dorsal fins are just visible slicing through the water. After going so long without spotting them, the sudden lightness I feel brings tears to my eyes.

They stay for an hour, perhaps searching for food. There are no boats in sight, and I feel like I'm alone with the whales. I watch through binoculars. As long as they're here, I'm not budging.

It gets dark, and I lose sight of their fins. But I stay to listen. Gradually, the sounds come closer. Whale breaths on all sides, like a surround sound theater. *Wait,* I think. *That sound like more than the dozen orcas I saw . . . way more.*

Then, to my left, I hear a tail hitting the surface of the water. And another to my right. *Slap . . . slap . . . slap!* Even without seeing them, I know it must be a super-pod. I can feel their joy. They haven't seen each other in ages, either. I listen with wonder as slaps echo around me in the darkness and the breaths keep time.

The next morning, the orcas are gone, back to the Pacific Ocean. But the local news confirms my hunch: that was a superpod. It brings a new glimmer of hope for me and many others—hope that these orcas can recover. It's not too late.

In this book, you'll meet the widely beloved Southern Resident orcas, from wise grandmothers to devoted moms and spunky youngsters. You'll also meet people in the human superpod fighting for their survival—people working as scientists, veterinarians, educators, policy advocates like me, and more. And whether you live near the Salish Sea, on the other side of the world, or somewhere in between, I invite you to join us.

Tahlequah:
17 Days and 1,000 Miles

In late July 2018, an orca named Tahlequah, age 20, gave birth. Calves are born tail-first because their tails and fins are floppy when they're in their mother's uterus. Coming out tail-first allows the cold ocean water to harden the fin, so the calf can swim to the surface and take a first breath.

But Tahlequah's baby didn't get to take many breaths. It is believed to have lived only 30 minutes at most. We'll never know exactly why it died.

Tahlequah, who scientists also refer to as J35, had one son already, eight-year-old Notch (J47). It's possible she'd had and lost other calves in the years since Notch was born, though researchers hadn't seen any. By the summer of 2018, three full years had passed without any of the Southern Residents having a successful birth and a calf that survived.

Tahlequah didn't let this new baby go. She balanced it on her head, pushing it up to the surface as if to help it breathe again. Sometimes she carried it in her mouth or on her back. When the calf's body slid off her head and began to sink, Tahlequah dove down to get it back.

People had seen mother orcas carrying dead calves in the past, but only for a few hours or a few days. Tahlequah far exceeded that. Day after day, the local news reported that Tahlequah still had the calf. Researchers surmised she was mourning, that it was emotionally hard for her to accept her baby was gone.

Pushing the 400-pound baby with her head was tough work. Tahlequah breathed heavily and fell behind her family as they swam. Focused on her calf, she didn't have the time or energy to catch salmon to eat. People began to worry she would die too.

At the time, I was taking a weeklong marine naturalist class at the Whale Museum on San Juan Island. The class was filled with people who loved orcas. They had traveled from South Dakota, Minnesota, Iowa, and even Denmark to learn all about these whales and try to catch a glimpse. As the seats filled up on the first day of class, I spotted tiny silver orcas dangling from the ears of a fellow student. Another young woman had an orca tattooed across her lower leg. A third person wore a brightly colored shirt with a repeating orca pattern. I later learned she had hand-sewn a different orca shirt to wear on each day of class.

The Whale Museum's director, Jenny Atkinson, stopped by each morning to give us updates on Tahlequah. Jenny looked exhausted and heartbroken. From sunrise to sunset, she was getting phone calls from reporters and was supporting her colleagues who were out on a boat making sure Tahlequah and her family had the space they needed to honor the calf.

"You can imagine her joy at meeting it, and then her reluctance to let go," Jenny told me later. "Maybe she was saying to her family, 'This baby is part of us, and I want to show our baby where we live—as much as I can, for as long as I can.' But we were trying to help the world understand what none of us really understood."

As the days wore on, Tahlequah brought the plight of the endangered orcas to the attention of people around the globe. There were articles and updates on television and in newspapers and magazines across the country, as well as in Canada and the United Kingdom. People felt it deeply. They posted on social media, wrote poems, made art inspired by Tahlequah, and stayed glued to the news.

A few times, Tahlequah was seen without her calf, and researchers thought she had finally let it go. Later, they saw she had it again. Perhaps her family members were taking turns carrying it for her, or maybe she dove to get it after it drifted down.

Then, on the 17th day, Tahlequah finally released the calf. She had carried its body through Pacific Northwest waters for more than 1,000 miles (1,600 km). Tahlequah may have felt ready to say goodbye. Or she may have had no choice.

"She carried it until it literally fell apart," Jenny said when we talked. She took a shaky breath and grabbed a tissue. I knew Jenny to be tough as a barnacle, but I also knew that all of us working to protect these orcas cared about them in a very deep and personal way. "It decomposed so much she couldn't carry it anymore," she continued.

Tahlequah was seen chasing salmon shortly after letting her calf go. Researchers were relieved she hadn't been too weakened by the prior 17 days. She could get strong again, both physically and emotionally, and hopefully live to have another calf.

Mother orcas may only have one baby every several years, typically starting around age 14 or 15. Each pregnancy lasts 16 to 18 months. While Tahlequah's journey of grief seemed unprecedented, at least in terms of what humans have witnessed, her calf's fate unfortunately was all too common. An orca can live as long as us humans, if given the chance. But half of all Southern Resident calves die before they're even born or before their first birthday.

Why is that?

One problem is pollution in the environment. These orcas spend a lot of time near cities and industrialized areas like Seattle and Vancouver, British Columbia, where the waters are especially dirty. Toxic chemicals get into the smallest animals in the ocean. As larger animals eat those chemical-laden small animals, over time the toxic chemicals accumulate in their systems in harmful amounts. Orcas, as the biggest predators, have bodies chock-full of these chemicals; the chemicals weaken their immune systems, making it harder to recover from being sick. The chemicals also get passed from orca moms to their calves.

But the main reason is Southern Residents are not getting enough food. If an orca can't eat enough during the long pregnancy to support herself and a healthy baby, her body may have to let the fetus go.

Phoenix swims alongside his mom, Tahlequah. *Danielle Carter*

Tahlequah's journey was tragic. But two years later, in September 2020, there was good news: Tahlequah had a new baby, swimming and rolling playfully alongside her. He was named Phoenix (J57), after the mythical bird that rose from the ashes—a name reflecting renewed hope for the Southern Residents.

What's in a Name?

A straight dorsal fin, about six feet tall, rises from the water. As 30-year-old Blackberry (J27) emerges, the white swoosh on his back is briefly visible. His distinctive white saddle patch—the pattern on an orca's back behind the dorsal fin—had a branch like a hooked finger. It made Blackberry one of the first Southern Residents I learned to recognize.

Blackberry takes a quick breath as his younger brother Mako (J39) comes up nearby. Mako's dorsal fin is a little shorter and curvier. Their sister Tsuchi (J31) appears alongside and gives a glimpse of her saddle patch, which is closed, or solid—not finger-shaped like Blackberry's.

Blackberry's fin towers above those of Tsuchi and other family members. *Danielle Carter*

Even in the moments they come up for air before slipping back under the surface, experts can recognize them by those unique characteristics.

It was a Canadian researcher, Dr. Michael Bigg, who first realized he could tell individual orcas apart, back in 1973. At first, few people believed him. But Mike, as he was known, soon proved it to be true. The Southern Residents each have a different saddle-patch pattern, rather like a fingerprint. The shapes of their dorsal fins also vary. And just like humans can have scars from injuries, some orcas have scratches on their bodies or nicks or notches along the edge of their dorsal fins.

Mike's realization opened a world of possibilities. Once scientists could identify individual whales, they could study their health, what happened to them, and how they interacted with each other. It let researchers gather information about birth rates, death rates, and the organization of the pods.

It also let us call these orcas by name.

~~~~~~~

Scientists refer to individual Southern Residents using "alpha-numerics," the letter of their pod and then a number. So, the first one named in J pod, Blackberry's father, was J1. Researchers also nicknamed J1 "Ruffles" because of his wavy dorsal fin. By the early 1980s, people had named all the Southern Residents.

Some people stick to using the alpha-numerics, like J27. They might say the name "Blackberry" makes the orca sound like a cute pet, not the wild animal he is. Or that the alpha-numeric system is more scientific.

Personally, I like to use both. "Blackberry" feels even more like a unique individual to me, with a personality and a family. The alpha-numeric reminds me how he fits into his community. He's part of J pod, and I know he was identified a while ago—and is therefore older—because his number is lower than the ones carried by the current youngsters.

Jenny Atkinson, executive director of the Whale Museum, understands that people have different

Names Hold Stories

In 1983, when there was a proposed capture of orcas in Canada for a marine park, the Whale Museum turned to names as a way to inspire people to protect the whales. Together with Greenpeace Victoria, they launched a contest to name the orcas in L pod. L22 became Spirit. L41 became Mega.

The Whale Museum decided to continue that work to build people's personal connection with orcas. Today, anyone who symbolically "adopts" an orca through their program gets to suggest names for new calves. The public votes.

Some calves are named after a distinctive marking; Notch has a healed wound on his dorsal fin. Calves born to Samish (J14) or her offspring have indigenous names given by the Samish Nation in traditional potlatch ceremonies. For example, the name of J37, Hy'Shqa, means "blessing" or "thank you."

Most adopters are kids. They often choose to adopt Oreo (J22)—named, of course, for an orca's classic black-and-white coloring—and her son Cookie (J38). The fun names make those orcas especially popular.

opinions about how to refer to these orcas, and ultimately, she says, it doesn't matter—as long as we're all treating them with respect.

~~~~~~~

The ability to identify individual Southern Residents is important for another reason. It makes it possible to

This is Notch. Can you spot the reason he got that name?
Danielle Carter

count exactly how many remain. The Center for Whale Research, led by Ken Balcomb, maintains an annual census of all the orcas and has collected photos to identify them since 1976. The census tells us exactly how many there are—or rather, how *few* there are—which helps us feel the urgency of saving them.

Before Mike and Ken started identifying individual Southern Residents and doing the census, there weren't exact counts. Populations of top predators are usually small, because they're at the top of their food chain, and it takes a lot of small- and medium-sized animals to support them. Estimates for what the Southern Resident population size may have been prior to the late 1800s range from 140 to 250.

Whatever that past number was, we know it began to drop in the late 1800s. Fishermen shot orcas because they thought they were scary and eating their catch. Southern Resident numbers dropped again, steeply, in the 1960s and 1970s, as many were taken for display in marine parks. In 1976, there were only 71 left in the wild.

Once people stopped shooting and capturing orcas, the population slowly grew but never approached pre-capture numbers. Canada listed the Southern Residents as endangered in 2003. The United States did so in 2005 when there were 82 remaining. Today there are fewer—73 at the time of writing. So few, the US government has listed Southern Residents as one of the nine marine species most at risk of extinction.

The Daily Special

Imagine you're a marine biologist and there's a mysterious new kind of whale discovered in the wild. Like other whales, they spend most of their time out of sight, underwater. Nobody knows what they're eating. It's your job to figure out their diet. You can only catch glimpses of them coming up to breathe, and you can't get close. How would you do it?

Perhaps start by standing on shore with a pair of binoculars. When the whales swim by, foraging for food, look for an orca bringing something to the surface. Can you see what's in its mouth?

If you're in a boat, you can try something else. Keep your distance and wait until the whale swims away, so as not to disturb it, then steer the boat over to look at the surface of the water where the whale had been. Are there any food scraps floating there, left behind after the whale's meal? Scoop up some samples.

Now, follow several hundred yards behind the whale. Collect some whale scat—poop—and analyze it in the lab to see what's in it. It's like dissecting an owl pellet in school and finding tiny mouse bones, but here you're looking at bits of fat and fish scales, not bones, and relying on more sophisticated lab equipment.

Finally, if someone reports a dead whale washed up on a beach, you can get your hands dirty to learn more. Put on safety equipment like gloves and goggles, then open up the carcass and look inside its stomach. Maybe you can tell what it ate before it died.

Nova (J51) and his mom, Eclipse (J41), catch a salmon. Taken under NMFS permit 19091. *Holly Fearnbach/SR3 and John Durban/NOAA*

Scientists with research permits have used all these methods to puzzle out the answer for the Southern Resident orcas. In the 1980s, they realized Southern Residents eat fish, while other orcas in the region eat marine mammals like seals and porpoises. In the 1990s and 2000s, scientists collected more data showing the Southern Residents are after a specific kind of fish: salmon. It makes up as much as 96 percent of their diet during some parts of the year.

And while there are several types of Pacific salmon—chum, pink, sockeye, coho, and Chinook—the Southern Residents don't go for just any of them. From studying scat and food scraps left on the water, researchers know they prefer Chinook (often called "king salmon" in grocery stores and on menus). While there are fewer Chinook available compared to other types of salmon, they're the biggest and have the most fat. Researchers estimate an adult orca needs 300 to 400 pounds of food per day. That's as many as 25 salmon, depending on how big the fish are.

~~~~~~~~~~

When you get hungry, you can probably find something to eat in the fridge. When an orca like Tahlequah gets hungry, she has to do a lot more work. She may spend a full half hour chasing one scrumptious salmon as it zips around the ocean to deep water and back up to the surface.

Whales or Dolphins? Both!

Some whales, like humpbacks, have baleen. Baleen is made of keratin, like your fingernails. It serves as a food filter in their mouth, straining tiny plankton out of the water.

Other whales have teeth and hunt larger animals. That category of toothed whales includes dolphins. Orcas are the largest dolphins, but they're still in the broader whale family. So, if you hear people arguing about whether orcas are dolphins or whales, you can say, "You're both right."

But there's something we do have in common with the orcas: we share our food. We pass the bread basket around the dinner table, we take soup to a sick friend, we split the last cookie.

When Tahlequah finally nabs a salmon with her teeth, she could easily eat it all in a flash, and she's hungry enough to do that. But she doesn't.

She comes up to the surface and shakes her head vigorously until the fish breaks into a few chunks. She

Family sticking together—Moby, Kiki, Tahlequah, and Notch. *Danielle Carter*

eats one piece while other orcas who have been waiting nearby—perhaps her sons, Notch and Phoenix, and her younger brother Moby (J44)—gobble up the rest.

One salmon is not too much for her to eat. Catching that particular fish wasn't a team effort that then requires sharing—she got it on her own. She isn't expecting Moby and Notch to necessarily share their fish in return. So why does she share?

For one thing, it could help her avoid having to compete with her own family for the scarce Chinook salmon. They don't all have to chase after the same fish and battle it out, which would take a lot of energy and perhaps cause injuries. They all know the one chasing the Chinook will share it.

Second, sharing food teaches young calves the best foods to eat. Every time Tahlequah tosses fish to little Phoenix, she's saying, "This is what food is; you'll learn to catch this someday."

And third, sharing fish helps the family survive and continue their genetic line, like all animals are hard-wired to do.

A study on Northern Residents, which have a similar culture and can tell us things about the Southern Residents as well, found that adult female orcas would share nine of every ten salmon they caught. These females shared mostly with their own calves under age five, but also sometimes with their sisters—perhaps as a thank-you for babysitting while they were busy chasing fish—and with nieces and nephews.

Youngsters are still learning to hunt and don't catch as many fish, so they probably can't afford to share the calories all the time. And yet, they still share two-thirds of the fish they catch, mostly with their mothers, brothers, and sisters.

Older males shared the least frequently—about one in four—with their mothers and siblings. That makes sense, because males are bigger and need to eat more than female orcas do. They also aren't on the receiving end of much of the sharing. When an adult male orca does receive food, it's likely to be from his mother or perhaps his grandmother.

Like other whales, orcas don't drink seawater. They get all the hydration they need from the fish they eat. When their body breaks down fat from the fish, that process makes water.

Salmon are born in rivers and swim downstream to the ocean. They live in the ocean for a few years, grow big, and then return to the same river where they were born to lay eggs and die.

The orcas have learned which kinds of salmon return to which rivers. They track down fish heading that direction at precisely the right times of year. For example, in the summer, orcas tend to visit the area off the west side of San Juan Island—which some people refer to as the "salmon highway"—in search of salmon returning to the Fraser River near Vancouver, British Columbia.

Salmon that used to migrate in some rivers are now completely gone, while other populations are in sharp decline. The salmon are also smaller than before. People are to blame: for removing water, destroying habitat, building dams, and changing the climate such that waterways can be too warm for fish to survive. As a result, the Southern Residents often don't have enough salmon to eat. But they still share what they catch with their families—and work to survive together.

The Salmon People

Coast Salish Tribes like the Lummi also depend on salmon. They're fighting to restore salmon to protect their way of life, as well as to protect the Southern Resident orcas and the Salish Sea.

"There hasn't been a generation in my family that hasn't fished since time immemorial," says Tah-Mahs, a Lummi Nation member. "We are the Salmon People, and it's going to be pretty sad to call ourselves the Salmon People if there are no more salmon."

In 2021, for example, Tah-Mahs was only able to fish for salmon for a few days. "It's not enough for me to survive on. And if it's not enough for me to survive on, it's not enough for our Southern Residents to survive on, either."

Tah-Mahs, on her fishing boat, talks about protecting salmon and the Salish Sea. *Courtesy of Sacred Sea*

Conversations Beneath the Waves

When Cookie was four, he swam off toward a boat trailing underwater microphones called hydrophones. His mom, Oreo, and big brother, DoubleStuf (J34), called to him in increasingly insistent tones, as if demanding he return. Cookie, in turn, sounded like a kid who was climbing a tree, higher than before, and didn't want to come down just because a grownup was getting nervous.

Dr. Scott Veirs, who coordinates the Orcasound network, was on the boat recording the calls. The Southern Residents keep up a regular chatter. We can't usually hear it from above the waves, but we can eavesdrop using hydrophones.

Normally, Scott says, the orcas like to be very close to each other. That makes it hard to figure out who is making which call. But on that relatively quiet day, only Cookie, Oreo, and DoubleStuf were around, and Cookie's wandering made it easy to pinpoint which calls were his.

"You can interpret it as the mother or the brother saying, 'Hey, come back, you're getting too far away,'" Scott tells me with a smile. "And you can almost see the calf shaking his head, the calls sounding like, 'I don't want to listen to you.'"

In addition to the hydrophones that Scott and other scientists take out on boats, there are a few permanent ones around the Salish Sea, capturing underwater sounds around the clock. Tuning in to Orcasound's live hydrophone feed, I hear waves, loud boat and ship noise, and occasional rain. Scott calls this the orcas' "soundscape." It's the sounds they hear wherever they go.

I sign up for alerts, so I won't miss orcas passing by those underwater microphones. It's exciting and intriguing when they do, their mysterious sounds breaking through the background noise. I hear orcas chirping like birds in a rainforest, squeaking like wet rubber gloves, and making fainter plaintive calls. And when I play recordings of the orca superpod gathering I watched above water the previous year, it's like joining an underwater party—a cacophony of squeaks, creaks, and high-pitched honks. Check out the Southern Residents' sounds for yourself at live.orcasound.net, where you can also sign up for alerts about chances to listen live!

The orcas learned all those calls from their mothers. Like newborn human babies, calves make a lot of random screams until they're two months old. Then they gradually pick up on their mother's vocalizations.

Musical Signatures

Collectively, the Southern Residents make about two dozen different calls. Some calls are made by only one or two pods. Researchers have heard others, like S10, across all three pods. (The "S" stands for "Southern Resident" in the orca call catalog that biologist Dr. John Ford created in the 1980s.)

There are also family favorites. J pod orcas often make the S1 call, a kind of rising and then suddenly falling squeak. K pod seems fond of S16, a short eerie trill. L pod's favorite, S19, is like a person whistling to get someone's attention. Experts can be pretty sure which pod is swimming by if they detect one of those three calls.

Scott listens to a live hydrophone feed. *Scott Veirs, Orcasound*

Even though orcas make the same calls as their mothers, they have their own voices. Think about how you can recognize the voice of a friend in the hall before you turn to see who's there, even if all your friend says is "Hey, what's up?" Similarly, scientists believe each orca has a slightly different tone, enabling orcas to tell each other apart underwater. While I can't tell individual orcas apart by their sounds, I can hear differences between the pods. To me, J pod orcas sound like squeaky doors. K pod orcas sound like mewing kittens, and L pod, like birds.

So what are they communicating with all these noises? Scientists say the calls don't seem like words in a human language, combined into sentences. Instead, orcas often repeat the same sounds. Southern Residents may use some calls to coordinate and stay in touch when the pod spreads out over a large area to search for salmon. And some calls and the way they're made may be tied to orcas' moods. When orcas are chasing each other and getting excited, for example, their calls often become quicker and higher pitched. That does seem rather humanlike; maybe you've found yourself using a different tone of voice when you're in the heat of a game or spot a friend you've missed.

Make Some Noise

Orcas don't use vocal cords or their mouths to make sounds like we do, nor do they need to release any air to make noise. Instead, an orca makes sounds using air sacs in its head, near the blowhole.

Baleen whales, like humpbacks, have two blowholes. Orcas and other toothed whales have only one. Scientists think the other nasal passage may have evolved into something that's now used for calls and echolocation instead.

We can learn a lot about the Southern Resident orcas just by listening to them. We know what pod they're in. When their sounds are picked up at one hydrophone and then another, we know what direction they're heading. And we can detect them on foggy days and at night, when they wouldn't be spotted from boats or from shore.

But there is a lot we still don't know. And there are times when people are especially eager to figure out what an orca might have been communicating.

In early 2010, hydrophones off San Juan Island picked up the sound of an orca calling. From shore, it was clear that Ruffles, with his trademark wavy dorsal fin, was the

Ruffles, with his distinctive dorsal fin. *Scott Veirs, Beam Reach*

only orca in the area. In his late 50s at the time, he was believed to be the oldest male in the Southern Resident community. Ruffles seemed to be alone.

"He was doing this very weird thing," Scott says, "repeating a relatively rare call, S42, over and over again in a very steady, almost rhythmic pattern."

Nobody knew what he was trying to communicate. "Was he pausing and trying to listen carefully? Was he lost and trying to find the rest of his pod?" Scott wonders. "It was the last time I heard him."

Ruffles went missing and was presumed dead later that year. We'll never know if those strange calls were a sign of things changing in his world.

There will probably always be mysterious moments like that one in orcas' underwater chatter. But Scott and other scientists are working to decipher what they can.

It takes many hours of listening to all the hydrophone recordings to find a moment when orcas called on their way by. College students from around the world, including from Mexico, India, Russia, and Ecuador, are helping Scott's team create computer technology to speed up this process. Together, they're building a machine that can listen to recordings and note which noises were made by an orca, amid all the noises made by ships, waves, and birds.

Kids and other members of the public—community scientists—are pitching in to help. They're listening to and labeling any sound clips the machine isn't sure about. That teaches the machine to be better at detecting orca

Give It a Try!

Scott says while some kids are good at visually recognizing orcas from their saddle-patch patterns and fins, others seem especially attuned to audio and able to easily identify signature pod sounds or even individual call types.

Listen to the most common calls used by orcas in J, K, and L pods at www.orcasound.net/learn/. Then, help Orcasound teach its machine to recognize orca sounds by tagging clips at https://orcasound.github.io/orcaal/.

sounds. All the tagged clips are then ready for scientists to analyze.

"What I've been doing is taking those acoustic events that humans or machines said were interesting, and then listening very carefully and slowly and measuring and labeling things," Scott says. "We're starting to get the tools to answer the burning questions: What are they saying, and what does it mean?"

While machines like this one are getting smarter really fast, Scott says, "it's quite common for humans to be the first to hear the faint calls. And there have been times when the machine has missed an event and humans got it. So, for the foreseeable future, there's definitely a role for community scientists to play as listeners."

The machines still can't distinguish between the calls of Southern Residents and other kinds of orcas, for example, or between J pod and K pod. Scott smiles and tells me, "Kids can do that easily."

It's a Date!

Dr. Michael Weiss from the Center for Whale Research is intrigued by the idea that Southern Residents might share complicated information through their calls.

"I've seen whales coordinate movements over a long distance in a way that seems like it could only have happened through planning," he says.

He tells me a story from a few months earlier, when J pod had been hanging out in the Salish Sea for a few days. Then K and L pods came in from the Pacific Ocean as well. Michael was watching K and L pods while the Whale Museum's Soundwatch Boater Education team was with J pod. They all

(continued on the next page)

saw the orcas start hurrying around the same time—heading to the same point.

"The Ks and Ls rounded the corner around Discovery Island and then just absolutely booked it up north like they knew J pod was there," Michael said. "There was land separating those pods, so they couldn't have been hearing each other. Somehow, both groups knew they had a date to meet each other right off Stuart Island."

Michael emphasizes that's anecdotal—one observation, not a rigorous scientific study. "But from my perspective, it seemed pretty clear they *planned* to some degree," he continues. "And the only way I can think of them communicating that plan is vocally. We don't know how that would be encoded, and we don't have any solid evidence, but I definitely don't rule it out as a possibility."

The Bonds of Family

Orcas are one of only eight mammal species on the planet—out of more than 5,000—that live in groups led by females.

A grandmother orca named Shachi (J19) is becoming the clear leader of J pod. The oldest female in the pod, she's a knowledge-holder, teacher, and caregiver. Shachi took over the J-pod job after the death of Granny (J2). Granny, with a distinctive half-moon-shaped notch in her dorsal fin, was almost always seen swimming out in front of the rest of the pod, deciding where they'd go. She was born well before researchers started doing the census, so nobody knew her exact age, but she was most likely over 70 years old and possibly over 100.

Even when a female orca like Granny or Shachi can no longer have babies, she can live another five decades. In the animal world, that's unique to orcas, a few other toothed whales like narwhals, and humans. Because older female orcas dedicate those years to supporting the younger orcas, they're vital to the pod's survival. When Granny was weakening at the end of her life, she was still taking care of the others; she was seen giving fish to a young orca who had recently lost his mother.

At the time of writing, the oldest orca in the Southern Resident community is a female in L pod, Ocean Sun (L25). She's believed to be in her nineties.

Shachi, in her early forties, is comparatively young. But she's ready to lead, teaching other J-pod orcas what she knows about where to find salmon in different seasons, and sharing the fish she catches.

Shachi, leader of J pod. *Cindy Hansen*

Shachi has a daughter named Eclipse (J41) and two grandchildren: a male, Nova (J51) and a female, Crescent (J58). When Nova was born, Eclipse was a very young mom, only 10 years old compared to a more typical age of 15. Many of the Southern Resident calves born that year didn't survive because Chinook salmon were in short supply. Grandma Shachi often stuck by little Nova's side when his mom went off to forage for food. He kept growing, likely thanks in part to his grandmother's care, in addition to the milk—40 percent fat—from his mom.

Nova is now seven years old. As he grows into an adult, he'll show us another thing that's special about Southern Resident families: their unshakeable bonds last a lifetime. He would have stopped nursing at age two or three, and he's had a few years to practice finding and catching salmon for himself. But he won't be striking out on his own. While many animals, including those from some other orca populations, would do just that, male and female Southern Residents stick by their moms for their entire lives. And because their moms have done the same thing, we see one big multigenerational family going everywhere together: kids, mothers, grandmothers, aunts, uncles, cousins.

These tight-knit families are built to survive. Their social structure helps them succeed in getting salmon, day in and day out. Because they stick together, they can rely on their mothers' and grandmothers' knowledge of where they've found salmon in the past. Their constant

The Lummi Nation, one of the Indigenous peoples of the Pacific Northwest, refer to orcas as *qwe 'lhol mechen,* meaning "our relations below the waves." "They put on a regalia that allows them to live under the water, but they are our relations," says Lummi Nation member Tah-Mahs.

communication, collaboration, and sharing also give them the best chance to all have a meal.

Nova will mate when he meets females in the Southern Resident community, and then return to his mom and grandma Shachi rather than sticking around with his own offspring. He will, however, help raise new nieces or nephews once his little sister Crescent is old enough to have babies. When Crescent is busy hunting salmon, Nova, Eclipse, and Shachi—who would be a great-grandma at that point—may all take turns babysitting.

It's very rare for Southern Resident orcas to move to different pods. But one orca has had to do it over and over.

Onyx (L87), born into L pod, lost his mother, Olympia (L32), when he was 13 years old. That's when his search for a new mother or grandmother figure began.

He moved to K pod, where he was adopted by leader Lummi (K7), whose own sons had died. When Lummi passed away, Onyx started traveling with her daughter Georgia (K11). Unfortunately, she died two years later.

Onyx had to shoulder that loss and move on, yet again. He went to J pod, where he was taken in by Spieden (J8). Spieden was nearly 80 years old, and after she died, Onyx began swimming with Granny. After Granny's death, Onyx finally returned to L pod, his original home. He'd had quite a journey, moving between pods for over a decade.

Onyx's search for an adoptive mother or grandmother was likely driven by the importance of social bonds as well as a survival instinct: if a mother orca dies, her male offspring under age 30 are three times more likely to also die within the next year. Those odds get

Onyx, born into L pod, tags along behind Blackberry, from J pod. *Danielle Carter*

worse when the sons are older. That may be because adult males are bigger and need more food—and thus benefit more from a salmon-sharing mom. When older females took Onyx in and shared their wisdom and their food, they helped make sure he'd live.

Connecting to other orcas beyond those older females would have been important too. Dr. Michael Weiss says male orcas get survival benefits from being well tied-in to a social network. "L87's [Onyx] finding a new family was really crucial—not just to find a new 'mom' or 'grandma' but to find a new family as a whole," he explains.

Kiki snuggles with big brother Moby. Taken under NMFS permit 21238. *Center for Whale Research/University of Exeter*

Onyx, now about 30 years old himself, experienced so many losses. But while he must have been no stranger to grief, I hope he has also felt the comfort of being welcomed and cared for, over and over. And I like imagining him in the rare superpod events when he gets to reunite with other orcas he swam with over the years.

~~~~~~~~~~

We have a lot in common with orcas. We recognize each other as unique individuals. We spend time with our grandmothers and learn from them. We share meals. We play and hang out together. We babysit. We snuggle our loved ones. We grieve when we lose someone we love.

And we stand by our families, even when it puts us in danger—like the danger the orcas faced half a century ago.

Dark History

In July 1970, more than 100 orcas from all three Southern Resident pods gathered in a joyous superpod near San Juan Island. The extended family was back together—youngsters, parents, aunts and uncles, grandmothers—to play, eat, and sing. Then, in early August, after hanging out for days, they gradually swam south together.

But the orcas weren't alone. A man named Ted Griffin was tracking them from a boat, following them day and night and radioing his colleagues.

These people weren't doing research.

They wanted whales.

The superpod arrived at a beautiful spot along Whidbey Island called Penn Cove. That's where Ted and his team, now with a bigger boat and a spotter plane, made their move. They surrounded about 50 Southern Residents, trapping them behind a net that stopped them from swimming back out into the open water.

Other Southern Residents were still free to go. But they didn't leave. Their family ties were too strong to abandon their relatives inside the nets. They stayed close.

Lifelong family bonds make the orcas strong in so many ways—they support each other and share food and knowledge—but in this situation, with people wielding a net, those bonds also made the orcas vulnerable. The captors seized the opportunity to trap approximately 40 more.

People came to see the orcas in Penn Cove, and for many, emotions shifted from excitement to dismay.

Trapped Southern Resident orcas in Penn Cove, 1970. *Department of Game photograph, Washington State Archives*

They reported hearing sounds like the orcas were crying. Meanwhile, the captors were deciding which ones to keep for marine parks, trying to separate them out from the rest, and making transportation plans.

As the days passed, at least five of the orcas got tangled in the nets. Unable to come up to the surface to breathe, they died. Ted's team released some of the others but held on to seven young whales.

One of those was a female orca between four and six years old, beloved by her L pod family. Her captors sold her for $20,000.

She was initially named Tokitae, but when she got to the Miami Seaquarium, she was given the name Lolita and taught to perform for paying visitors. She met another Southern Resident there, Hugo, who had been captured two years earlier.

~~~~~~~

As I write this book, this orca is still at the Miami Seaquarium, the only captured Southern Resident orca who is still alive. For over half a century, she performed tricks twice a day. She hasn't interacted with another orca since Hugo died in 1980. But people are speaking up for her, and the Lummi Nation has given her a new name, Sk'aliCh'elh-tenaut (*SKAH-lee CHUCK-ten-NUT*).

"She's just in this teeny tank—she can never get up to full speed," says Tah-Mahs, a member of the Lummi Nation. "It's heartbreaking."

Sk'aliCh'elh-tenaut in her tank. *Courtesy Anonymous*

Many believe Sk'aliCh'elh-tenaut is related to and possibly the daughter of Ocean Sun, the oldest living Southern Resident at the time of this writing. In the wild, Sk'aliCh'elh-tenaut would have stayed with her mother for her whole life.

Tah-Mahs knows Sk'aliCh'elh-tenaut has not forgotten her family. "She still sings the Southern Resident songs," Tah-Mahs tells me. "That she's had the strength to endure what she has gone through for 51 years—in the tiniest tank, in the sun, nowhere near home, with no companion whatsoever of her own kind—just proves how strong she is."

In 2021, government inspectors expressed concerns that Sk'aliCh'elh-tenaut wasn't getting enough food and had been fed rotten fish. Paint was flaking off into the pool and there wasn't enough shade to protect her from the sun. Trainers made her do big jumps and fast swims even though she was old and had injuries from hitting her jaw in shows or training sessions.

Some changes were made to address specific violations. But Sk'aliCh'elh-tenaut is still living in that small pool.

The Lummi Nation, along with members of the public and organizations like Orca Network and the Center for Whale Research, has been campaigning for years for Sk'aliCh'elh-tenaut to be released and brought back to her home waters. They've organized protests, threatened to file lawsuits, and sent letters to the Miami Seaquarium. The Lummi journeyed across the country with a cedar totem pole carved by Jewell Praying Wolf James and Doug James to bring more awareness to the orca's plight. So far, the Miami Seaquarium hasn't budged.

Tah-Mahs won't either. "Our chief was very clear in telling us that Sk'aliCh'elh, the orcas, are our relatives under the sea. He told us we needed to protect them," she explains. "And to make the Southern Residents whole again means we have to return the daughter that we allowed to be stolen 51 years ago. Her mother is still out there, swimming, and we'd like to bring her back to her waters where her family is."

Sk'aliCh'elh-tenaut is over 55 years old now. She could have a few decades of life left. Will that life be lived in a small tank in Miami?

Being flown across the country and transitioning back into the Salish Sea could be taxing and even dangerous for Sk'aliCh'elh-tenaut, if not done carefully. But the Lummi Nation and their partners have been working on a detailed plan and continue to fight to get her returned to the Salish Sea—and to her family—before she dies.

"There's something that's keeping her going," Tah-Mahs tells me. "She possesses something that is making her strong. We won't stop fighting. We'll keep trying until we get her home."

<hr />

The 1970 capture in Penn Cove was far from the only time people tore wild orcas from their families. In the 1960s and 1970s, marine parks around the world clamored to buy orcas taken from the waters of Washington and Canada. The price of an orca kept rising—from $5,000 to as much as $75,000 by 1973 (the equivalent of over $450,000 today). At the time, a marine park with an orca got a lot of visitors paying to see it.

During the first few years of capturing orcas for marine parks, no permit was needed. Anyone could go out and corral an orca and sell it to the highest bidder. Ted Griffin, owner of the early Seattle Marine Aquarium (which closed in 1977), was one of the people who saw a business opportunity.

As demand from marine parks grew, hundreds of orcas were driven into shallow bays in Washington and

Canada and surrounded by nets. The Southern Residents, swimming in waters near population centers like Seattle and Vancouver, Canada, were easiest to find and get to an airport, and thus at the highest risk. The captors also preferred to take younger orcas because they were smaller, easier to move, and easier to train.

Some of the trapped orcas were released because they weren't the right size. Some got tangled in the nets while trying to escape or reach their trapped calves. Once entangled, they drowned because they couldn't come up for air. Some orcas escaped, though many of those were likely caught again later. And ultimately, more than 50 orcas were separated from their families and sold. They were shipped to marine parks all over the world: Seattle,

Orcas captured in Penn Cove, August 1971. *Department of Game photograph, Washington State Archives*

Vancouver, New York, Texas, Florida, California, France, Great Britain, Japan, Australia, and Germany.

At first, people who had captured or bought orcas didn't know how to keep them alive. They knew little about how to move orcas safely, what they ate, or what conditions could harm their health. The first orca ever displayed publicly, after being taken from California waters, died less than two days after her capture in 1961. She was dropped and hit her head while being moved into a pool, and then she rammed the sides over and over while she swam. Others died because they were kept in pens with sewage runoff from Seattle or freshwater run-off from a river near Vancouver. One died after eating a stick tossed by a visitor. For the first several years, all the captured orcas—who should have had decades of life left—died within 12 months.

Eventually, captures weren't quite as much of a free-for-all. Canada began requiring permits in 1966, and Washington did the same in 1971. But permits weren't hard to get; there might just have been some restrictions. Washington State, for example, told Ted Griffin's company not to hold orcas in nets for more than 10 days or keep any orcas shorter than 8 feet or longer than 16 feet.

Seeing orcas in marine parks and aquariums changed how people thought about them. Instead of being afraid, people became fascinated. Those close-up experiences helped change how the public thought about orcas. They contributed to today's widespread belief that the

orcas are worth protecting and saving. But that's no jus-
tification for the captures.

The orcas taken from the waters of Washington and
Canada included an estimated 47 Southern Residents—
one-third of the wild population. That was almost an
entire generation. It meant the loss not only of those individual whales, but also the calves they would have had if
left in the wild. The captures were a horrific tragedy and
a cause of the Southern Residents' ongoing struggles.

~~~~~~

I work at an aquarium. It's one that has never had a
whale, and that's driven by a mission of inspiring conservation. My colleagues and I work hard on education
and policy programs that we hope can contribute to the
recovery of these endangered orcas.

Still, the fact that marine parks were responsible for
the original decline of the Southern Resident orcas, years
ago, sometimes feels like it hits close to home. Some of
the capture events involving J, K, and L pods were also
literally close to my home; while they happened before
I was born, they would have been visible from the small
island near Seattle where I grew up and where I live
again now.

Back in the 1960s, some residents were initially excited
when they saw orcas up close in the nets. Ralph Munro,
who later became Washington's secretary of state,
remembers being on a bridge with 10,000 people who

were cheering when Ted Griffin went underneath, towing a whale in a pen, headed for the Seattle waterfront.

But that feeling changed over time. Shifting perspectives about the environment, whales, and animal welfare were reflected in the organization of the first Earth Day in 1970 and the passage of the Marine Mammal Protection Act in 1972.

March 1976 was a turning point in Washington State. One Sunday afternoon, Ralph Munro, then aide to Republican Governor Dan Evans, was out sailing near Budd Inlet, which is close to Olympia, the state capital. "We saw some whales come down the bay," he recounts. "I thought they were going a little too fast—it just didn't look quite right, and they were kind of grouped together, and they were way in shallow water."

Then Ralph realized there was a boat chasing them, as well as an airplane. People were using explosives to drive orcas deep into the harbor. The orcas, not Southern Residents this time, tried to swim out. But the captors, who were working under a SeaWorld permit, had strung up a net and closed it around six of them.

"It was pretty gruesome," Ralph says. "There were family members of the pod outside, family members inside, screaming back and forth." Over four decades later, he says he can still hear those screams.

Ralph called a reporter. The next day, it was front-page news. Soon, crowds of protestors gathered in kayaks and canoes and on the beach near the corralled orcas. Meanwhile, Ralph worked with his boss—the

An orca captured in Budd Inlet in 1976 is loaded into a sling.
Department of Game photograph, Washington State Archives

governor—and the state attorney general to figure out what to do. SeaWorld had a legal permit, but Washington State still filed a lawsuit against them, arguing the capture methods were inhumane. The effort succeeded: in the end, SeaWorld agreed to never again seek permits or capture whales in Washington State waters.

Of the six orcas netted in Budd Inlet for SeaWorld, three managed to escape. One was released because he was too big to legally keep. The final two, which scientists later decided were probably a mother and son, were temporarily given—with the judge's permission—to a researcher, who released them the following month with radio packs. SeaWorld, which was desperate for new orcas to be attractions at their marine parks, left the state empty-handed.

Marine parks didn't give up. Displaying orcas was big business. But public opposition to orca captures in Washington State and Canadian waters was intensifying. By 1980, marine parks were taking orcas from around Iceland instead. The capture era hadn't ended, but the pressure was off the Southern Residents.

~~~~~~~

Science was essential to stopping the captures. Previously, some people had argued the state couldn't limit the number of whales that could be captured because it didn't even know how many were out in the ocean. Dr. Mike Bigg's work changed that. When he proved it was possible to identify individual Southern Resident orcas using their markings and scars, he made it possible to do a more precise count of the population.

Mike organized the first orca census in 1971, recruiting hundreds of volunteers in the United States and Canada to count every orca they saw, all on the same day. As it turned out, people had been estimating there were three times as many Southern Resident orcas as there actually were.

The dark history of capture also carries both a lesson and inspiration for me as a policy advocate. Orcas were taken because for a long time, no laws forbade it. And then a permitting process made capture explicitly acceptable, with few restrictions. But policy was ultimately also critical to stopping it.

Art in Action

"I was kind of known as the orca kid when I was in middle school," Taylor Redmond says with a smile.

For a class project, she and her friends learned about Tokitae (or Sk'aliCh'elh-tenaut) at the Miami Seaquarium. Then Taylor did something even bigger: she created a mural inside the school, with Tokitae as one of six orcas she chose to paint.

"I wanted to bring awareness to my grade that these are really struggling orcas,

Taylor visits the mural she painted in her middle school. *Dawn Redmond*

(continued on the next page)

and we are playing a part in their plight," she explains.

Now that she's in high school, Taylor is finding new ways to help the Southern Residents. She uses her photos to learn to identify individual orcas and shares her photos—and facts about the orcas—on her Instagram feed (@eclipse_j41). She and her mom also sell T-shirts printed with her art to raise money for orca conservation organizations.

"I really like to use art, whether it be drawing or photography, to help express my interest in whales," she says.

The Canadian government passed a law in 1970 banning the capture and killing of orcas except under limited permits issued to Canadians. And in 1975, Greenpeace and others lobbied and secured a moratorium, or temporary prohibition, on any orca capture in Canadian waters. In the United States, the Marine Mammal Protection Act helped restrict capture permits that same decade.

People made a difference by speaking up and protesting. Legislators don't pass laws unless they hear widespread support. And the Marine Mammal Commission finally declared its opposition to orca captures in Puget Sound based on one key reason: "It bothers people."

This directly inspires my own work as a policy advocate: speaking up matters. Right now, I'm asking legislators to put more money toward salmon recovery, so the orcas have more to eat. I'm calling for new boating laws, so the orcas have more space and quiet.

I'd like to think I wouldn't have hesitated in the earliest days to protest the capture of these magnificent, intelligent, social beings. But today, I have the opportunity, like we all do, to speak up about the threats preventing the Southern Residents from recovering from their decade of loss—and about what we must do now to help.

From the Air

How do you measure an orca swimming out in the sea? You can't catch it and put it on a scale. It won't hold still while you line up your measuring tape.

One solution sounds like an action movie. Picture this: two intrepid scientists in a loud helicopter hover 1,000 feet (300 m) above a pod of orcas. The helicopter has no door. The first scientist, Dr. Holly Fearnbach, leans out the opening, while Dr. John Durban sits in the front seat helping the pilot track the animals. Holly holds a camera as steady as she can and takes photos straight down at the tops of the whales as they surface.

This action-movie scenario was real. It sounds scary to me. When I ask Holly, she says there was always the risk of a crash, as with any aircraft. But she had a seat belt and harness to keep from falling when she leaned out the door with the camera. And she focused on her goal: collecting images she could use to measure the whales.

Why does an orca's size matter, anyway? Well, if you can figure out how long or how fat orcas usually are, you can use that information to evaluate how individuals are doing. If a female orca is skinnier than she was the year before, for example, she might be malnourished or sick. Understanding the health of individual whales also lets Holly and John assess the health of the overall population.

For decades, the only data on size and health came from dead orcas found on beaches or captured orcas measured to see if they were the right size to be legally kept for marine parks. Aerial photos taken from a helicopter were a solution, though not a perfect one.

"Helicopter flights are very expensive," Holly says when we chat. She works for an organization called Sealife Response + Rehabilitation + Research (SR3), and John works for Southall Environmental Associates, Inc. They could only afford to take one flight a day, usually lasting just over an hour.

A few years later, the action-movie setup was replaced by a tamer but still fascinating sequel: Holly and John use camera-carrying drones. Drones are much quieter than helicopters, less expensive to use, and safer to operate. Nobody has to lean out an open window high above

Holly and John retrieve a drone used to photograph whales. Research conducted under NMFS permit 19091. *NOAA, SR3, Vancouver Aquarium*

the water amid thundering noise. And they can stay out all day if needed to capture enough usable images of all the whales.

These days, Holly and John ride on a small research boat and try to stay at least 200 yards (180 m)—two football fields—away from the orcas to avoid disturbing them. John flies the drone toward the whales at an altitude of more than 100 feet (30 m), as high as a seven-story building. Meanwhile, Holly studies the live video feed from the drone's camera, a towel draped over her head and the ground station screen to block sun glare. She monitors the drone's battery and altitude and gives directions to John.

"It's in the middle of the frame," Holly calls to John as she catches sight of an orca on the video feed. "Just try to hold, go slowly, go to the right, slowly to the right, OK good . . . come down a little, OK she's back in the middle, she's coming up, she's going to be in the middle [of the frame], she's good."

As soon as John gets the drone over a whale, he triggers the camera to start taking photos—up to two per second.

The team collects aerial images throughout the year. They avoid windy days because choppy water makes it hard to clearly see and measure the whales' bodies.

"We need really flat water and nice water clarity," Holly explains. "In the spring, the water is often much greener. Runoff from the Fraser River makes things murky, and it's hard to see the edges of the whales."

Even when weather and water conditions are perfect, only a few of the photos will be usable. A whale's body needs to be oriented straight, not tilted to one side or the other, which Holly can confirm by seeing the same amount of white eye patch on each side of its head. But it's not like Holly and John can give the whales stage directions. They just have to take a lot of photos.

Back at her computer, Holly pulls the best shots of each whale. She matches the saddle-patch patterns to an aerial catalog of Southern Residents to determine whose portraits they have just taken. Then she takes careful measurements. Do any of the orcas look skinny? Did an orca's condition change over time? Which orcas are in the most trouble? Are any of them pregnant?

Holly and John may take more than 100,000 photos in a year. If those were all printed out index-card size and laid side by side, they'd stretch nearly eight miles. It takes months to analyze everything. But the first order of business is looking at the eye patches. "If the eye patches are angled outwards, they have a lot of fat behind their skull and are in good, robust condition," Holly explains. "If the eye patches are angled more straight down, the whale might be on the leaner side. If the eye patches start

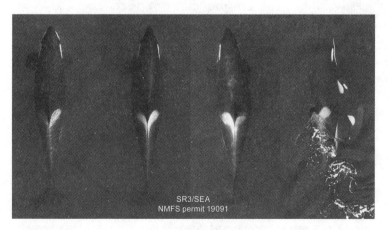

SR3/SEA
NMFS permit 19091

Tahlequah's growing pregnancy, as seen from the drone, resulting in the arrival of baby Phoenix. Taken under NMFS permit 19091. *Holly Fearnbach/SR3 and John Durban/Southall Environmental Associates*

Caution, Baby on Board!

In 2021, Holly and John reported they'd seen three J pod orcas in the late stages of pregnancy. It was happy and exciting news, but tinged with worry, given that many pregnancies fail. The state passed an emergency rule requiring whale-watching boats to stay half a mile away and urged other boaters to do the same. The local news reported on the need to protect these three orcas and give them more space to find food. In 2022, we learned Hy'Shqa had a new baby girl, but the pregnancies of Shachi and Alki (J36) hadn't succeeded. By continuing to merge science with policy and broader public action, hopefully we can give new calves and their moms a brighter future.

angling inwards, often tracing the shape of the skull, it's because the whale has lost that fat behind the head, and they're in very poor condition."

They also look at changes in body condition over time. Comparing the width of 44 orcas' heads over the course of five years, Holly and her team found 11 whales got noticeably skinnier—all females at the right age to be having babies—and two died shortly thereafter. They concluded that if an orca's body condition gets measurably worse, that can be an early warning that it's at high risk of dying. The results also indicated many nursing orca moms need more food than they're getting; it takes a lot of energy to make milk. Holly and John hope their research can be used to help save whales before they die.

Aerial photos also showed orcas weren't growing to be as long as their older relatives. In fact, the younger adults are about 1 foot (0.3 m) shorter. Holly and John suggested these shorter orcas didn't get enough to eat when they were young, stunting their growth.

Now, Holly and John are working with a team that's making a tool to help them track whales' body conditions using artificial intelligence, meaning it will perform some human-like tasks and learn from experience. The goal is for it to identify and measure individual whales, so that people do not have to do that time-consuming work.

"We have to train the tool," Holly says. "It's machine learning. But it would be tremendous to get the photo analysis down from six months to six weeks or even faster."

Continuing to measure orcas' sizes and growth will also help show whether actions taken to increase salmon abundance—like restoring salmon habitat or changing fishing regulations—are in fact creating more food for the orcas and improving their body condition.

A Flying Whale

Research drones aren't the only things help-ing orcas from the air. Pilots Michael Hays and Anna Gullickson had a Kenmore Air seaplane painted in black and white—like a flying whale—to raise awareness about the orcas' plight.

The Wild Orca seaplane. *Christopher S. Teren*

The Wild Orca Seaplane carries about 10,000 people per year in the skies above the orcas' home waters. Whether passen-gers are traveling for work or vacation, when this seaplane pulls up at the dock, it's a fun surprise. More importantly, it inspires people

(continued on the next page)

to learn about the endangered orcas—and to act.

There are so many things we can all do to help these whales, from writing letters to our elected officials to thinking twice about what we buy. Flip to the back of this book for ideas.

Holly says she has the best job because she has the best view. And the bird's-eye view of what the orcas are doing is incredible. "We see whales socializing and young calves nursing. We see foraging events—the youngsters aren't very good at catching salmon, and they'll go around in circles. The mom will come in and snatch it up and break it apart for them."

Holly loves being able to see those things. "But the reason *why* we do this research is to aid in the recovery of the population."

Several government agencies and organizations in both the United States and Canada use the health metrics Holly and John provide. When Holly and John spot individual whales that look malnourished or sick, they also share that information with other scientists and veterinarians who could potentially help. That kind of intervention happened for the very first time in 2018, with a young orca named Scarlet.

Whale Doctors

On a sunny day in late July 2018, a pod of Southern Resident orcas swam by San Juan Island. Watching from shore, I spotted a boat approaching one of the orcas, closer than regulations allow. Someone on the boat leaned over with a long pole. Who was it? A film-maker with a camera trying for a great shot? Was that legal?

It turned out to be a team of scientists with a petri dish on a pole and a permit to let them get close. They were trying to help a four-year-old orca named Scarlet (J50) who was having a hard time swimming as fast as her siblings. She was too thin. Her breath smelled bad. But nobody was sure what was wrong.

Government agencies and organizations from the United States and Canada were tracking Scarlet's condition. In the field, two veterinarians, Dr. Marty Haulena of the Vancouver Aquarium and Dr. Joe Gaydos of the SeaDoc Society, were her primary medical team.

"It was immediately obvious there was something wrong," Marty told me later.

For the first time, the US government had authorized wildlife vets to treat a free-ranging endangered orca. And Marty and Joe desperately wanted to save her.

Joe notes that a healthy population isn't about saving every single animal. "That's not the way nature works. Animals get eaten; animals get old. But when you go out and see a young animal that's really, really sick, and you're worried it's related to something that people have caused, it gives you that visceral feeling of *Man, I really want to help.*"

In a very small population like the Southern Resident orcas, the health and survival of individuals—especially young females like Scarlet who could grow up to have babies and help the population grow—is vital.

Joe and Marty went out on boats to observe how Scarlet was acting, looking through binoculars to give her as much space as possible. "It's helpful for us to look at how whales breathe, how they surface," Joe says. "It gives us clues about what is going on."

But they needed more information than they could get by watching Scarlet swim. They studied drone photos from Dr. Holly Fearnbach and Dr. John Durban.

Scarlet had always been small for her age. But now she seemed to have lost about 20 percent of her body weight compared to the year before. Scarlet probably wasn't getting enough fish to eat.

Joe and Marty wondered if that was the only problem, or if she was sick too. To try to find out, they needed a sample to analyze in the lab. If the sample contained any bacteria or fungus, that could explain Scarlet's condition. But they couldn't take a blood sample from a free-ranging whale without running the risk of harming her. Instead, they collected a breath sample with the petri dish on a pole I saw from shore. Unfortunately, the sample was too small, and lab testing didn't reveal bacteria pointing to a specific medical problem.

Other scientists tried to test her scat. A rescue dog from the Conservation Canines program was able to

Scientists collect a breath sample from Scarlet on July 21, 2018. Taken under NMFS permit 21368. *Katy Foster/NOAA Fisheries*

sniff out scat samples from Scarlet's family group for researchers to scoop up. Of course, it was hard to know which orca the scat came from. But DNA tests soon showed some of it was from Scarlet's mother, and it had parasites in it. Marty and Joe thought if her mother had parasites, Scarlet was likely carrying the same ones because they shared their food. While parasites probably weren't the main reason for Scarlet's deteriorating health, they might have been making it worse.

Time was running out. Joe and Marty had to start treatment, even though Scarlet's illness was still a mystery. In the past, when scientists studied other orcas that had died, they often found signs of bacterial pneumonia, a kind of lung infection. That made Joe and Marty think Scarlet could have pneumonia too, and so they decided to give her antibiotics. They would also give Scarlet a dewormer to help her get rid of any parasites. While they couldn't be sure these medicines would help, they had to try.

The aerial photos helped estimate Scarlet's body weight, so Joe and Marty could give her the right doses. Bigger animals need more medicine than smaller ones, just like adults need more medicine than kids.

Finding the patient was the next challenge. "We didn't know where Scarlet was going to go and when," Joe recalls. "We spent a lot of time at home waiting to go out on call."

They worried Scarlet would be getting skinnier and sicker by the day. "It was a very intense, anxious time," says Marty.

Scarlet with her family on August 9, 2018. Taken under NMFS permit 18786. *Katy Foster/NOAA Fisheries*

Finally, in early August 2018, Scarlet and her family were spotted again. The medical and science teams quickly prepared for long days on the boat.

Giving Scarlet the medicine wouldn't be easy. She was always on the move and getting too close or trying to catch her would be harmful. Joe and Marty also didn't want to separate her from her family.

They decided to see if Scarlet could be fed a fish that had her medication in it. The Lummi Nation pitched in for the test run. When Scarlet fell behind her group, the Lummi dropped a live salmon in her path using a long plastic tube, so it would appear in the water far behind the boat. That way, Scarlet wouldn't learn to approach boats for food.

Live salmon are released ahead of Scarlet from a Lummi Nation boat on August 12, 2018. Taken under NMFS permit 18786. *Candice Emmons/NOAA Fisheries*

Scarlet didn't seem to change direction to chase any of the swimming salmon. The water was too rough to see if she'd left behind pieces of gnawed fish. Nobody knew if she'd gone for it.

Given that the live fish tactic hadn't clearly worked, Marty and Joe decided to give Scarlet shots of antibiotics using a dart gun. SeaWorld vets shared what they knew about the dosage and needle size that would work best for an orca.

Can you imagine shooting a heavy dart from a moving boat into a swimming whale with thick, rubbery skin? And knowing you must hit a part of the whale's body where the medicine will work and not cause any harm? That's tricky, even for experts like Marty and Joe.

"You have to wait for the perfect conditions," Marty tells me. "The seas have to be relatively calm, there has to be very little wind, the visibility has to be good, and the whales have to be moving in a steady fashion. And the animal is at the surface for only a split second—she

Relatives Beneath the Waves

The Lummi Nation knew they had to help Scarlet. As a Southern Resident orca, she was family.

The Lummi chief, chairman, and several Tribal members went to a beach and lit a fire. They spoke to their ancestors and spirits and asked for permission to help the orcas. Then they boated to a chosen spot, sang songs, and placed a live Chinook salmon in the water as a ceremonial feeding for the orcas.

"That was our way of letting them know we are aware of their plight; we are aware of what's happening to them," said Tribal member Tah-Mahs. "It's not something that can be fixed in a day."

pops to the surface and pops back down. Treating her was almost an impossibility to begin with. There are a million and a half things that can go wrong."

On Marty's first try, he was able to hit Scarlet with the dart, but it fell out before all the antibiotics went into her body. On another day, Joe went out to give Scarlet a dewormer shot to help get rid of any parasites. He shot the dart but wasn't sure if he hit Scarlet. She regrouped with the other orcas and swam away.

A month into the effort to save Scarlet, at the beginning of September, her family was seen without her. Orca families stick together, so Marty and Joe knew that was a bad sign. Scientists went out searching.

Marty, in front, heads out to give Scarlet antibiotics with a dart gun on August 9, 2018. Taken under NMFS permit 18786. *Katy Foster/NOAA Fisheries*

Then Scarlet was spotted again, back with her family. Everyone was relieved. Marty prepared to give her more medicine. He adjusted the dart and the speed for the second treatment. It seemed to work better, though Marty still saw a bit of the medicine spray out the side when the dart hit Scarlet.

After that, a few days passed with no sign of Scarlet or her family. The team assumed they were swimming off the coast. They waited anxiously for the orcas to return to the inland waters of Washington.

Scarlet's family reappeared a week after her second treatment. Scarlet wasn't with them. The US Coast Guard, local airlines, and scientists all went out to try to find her.

On September 15, eight days after she was last seen, the US government ended their search. Scarlet was presumed dead. Everyone who had been working to help Scarlet was devastated.

"We all knew our chances of success were quite slim from the get-go," Marty tells me. "But we really, really wanted it to work."

Marty and Joe take some comfort in having learned from this first-ever attempt to treat a wild Southern Resident orca. They're already working on better response tools using those lessons.

When Scarlet was sick, for example, several different researchers had information about her, from past sightings and aerial photographs to hormone data. The vets had to hurry to collect it all, so they could figure out how to treat her. Now, Joe is helping to make health records for every Southern Resident. Vets and other scientists will be able to monitor the orcas' health over time and immediately access vital information on any that are unwell.

"We were guessing with Scarlet," says Joe. "If and when we go out and do it again, we will be starting at a better level."

Hopefully that won't be necessary. But if it is, they'll be ready.

Mystery of the Breach

Years ago, my dad and I went to Lime Kiln Point State Park at dawn. There were no other park visitors at that hour—nobody else to witness the orcas approaching from the south, or what happened next.

As we stood on the rocks, one of the passing orcas suddenly jumped high out of the water in front of us, at the edge of the kelp. It was enormous and unbelievably close—perhaps 15 yards away (14 m). I could see the bulk of its body as it took to the air. My heart nearly stopped from sheer wonder. As the orca landed on its side with a huge splash and disappeared underwater, I knew that moment would be stamped into my memory forever. And I was left with burning questions. What was going

Mega does a mega breach. *Danielle Carter*

through that orca's mind? Why, exactly, do orcas breach like that?

I'm not the only one who has stood on that rocky shoreline asking those kinds of questions. Dr. Bob Otis, a behavioral psychology professor from Wisconsin, has been coming to Lime Kiln every summer for over 30 years. He notes what the orcas are doing as they swim by—breaching, tail-slapping, hunting, resting, and more—and figures out how those activities relate to what's going on around them.

Bob and his research assistants do their work from the coolest office ever: a little lighthouse. I stop by to visit one summer morning. Set right next to the water, the lighthouse is a cute, creaky building that's usually chilly inside but has an amazing view.

When the orcas appear, the team runs out of the lighthouse and onto the rocks. They write down how many orcas they see and what they're doing. The whales' antics are still exciting, even after watching them hundreds or even thousands of times.

"There's an adrenaline rush that comes through your body every time you see these whales," says one of the researchers, Stephanie Dawes. She calls her summer work at the lighthouse a passion project. "You have split seconds to document things."

And why *do* orcas breach? There's no simple answer. But Bob and his team have gathered a lot of clues.

First, they've found these acrobatics are more common when there are two or three pods of Southern Residents hanging out together, rather than just one. Maybe the breach is part of their socializing or play.

Orcas are also more likely to breach and slap their tails when they're being aggressive. I imagine it's like a whale's version of hitting a punching bag.

Bob's team also found that Southern Residents passing the lighthouse tend to breach more often in late June—coinciding with more Chinook salmon in the area—compared to weeks in May or July. So breaching may also be a foraging trick. I wonder if breaching helps an orca startle, stun, or herd the salmon they want to catch.

Breaching and tail-slaps are also more common when orcas are waking up from a rest—perhaps like humans stretching as they get out of bed.

There's one more important reason why orcas might breach or slap their tails or fins: those moves make loud slaps and visible splashes. So, when it's too noisy for orcas to easily call or whistle to each other, they have another way to get each other's attention and communicate.

That idea is supported by evidence that orcas do these things more often when whale-watching tours and other boats come close. Maybe the orcas are warning each other that boats are nearby. Maybe they're trying to alert the boaters that whales are around. Or maybe the orcas are just trying to stay coordinated as a group amid the hubbub. That's one reason Bob does his research from shore: he doesn't have to worry about affecting the orcas' behavior. If he was in a boat, he might cause the orcas to breach more than they otherwise would, and that would change the results of his study.

When orcas sleep, they keep half of their brains awake, so they remember to come up for air. Researchers have found that orcas rest less often in the daytime now than they did 50 years ago, when there were fewer boats around to disturb them.

Looking back on three decades of research, Bob thinks the orcas probably use each of these behaviors for different purposes, depending on the situation. That makes sense; for a comparison, think about reasons you might wave your hand. Maybe you want to get someone's attention, say goodbye, or shoo away a mosquito. While the wave wouldn't be for the same reason every time, the context could provide clues to anyone watching.

When my dad and I saw the orca breach at dawn, there were no boats around. It was quiet. Commotion from boats wouldn't explain what we observed.

Playing detective, I ask my dad what he remembers. He says the orcas were so close we could see the black and white of their bodies underwater as we looked down. And then he recalls they had been all lined up as they headed our way.

"Side by side?" I hurry to ask. I hadn't remembered that, but now, with everything I've learned from Bob's research, I realize it's a potentially big clue about why that orca breached. Orcas sometimes swim in a line like that, surfacing to breathe and going down again in slow unison. The sight always reminds me of synchronized swimmers or a parading army. They do that when they're sleeping.

So the orcas we saw that early morning were probably resting. It seems likely that as they approached Lime Kiln, at least one of them was finished napping—and was inspired to do a waking-up breach right in front of us. But I can't say the case is closed because I'll never

know for sure. Maybe, instead, the orca was feeling playful or aggressive. Or maybe there was another motiva-
tion that we can't guess yet.

Bob's favorite reason for orcas breaching out of the
water came from talking to a class of fourth graders. He
smiles at the recollection. "One said maybe it's so the
whale can dry off."

Bob says these kinds of reflections about orca behavior are useful. Kids can help scientists see and think about
things in new ways. "We usually ignore the importance
of observation, but kids can be really good at it."

"There's a behavior we don't have a name for, when a
mother orca pushes her young one above the surface of
the water," Bob continues. "A kid said we should call it
'Monday morning.'" I laugh, remembering the struggles
of getting up for school, especially on dark fall days.

In addition to figuring out when orcas are *more* likely
to breach, Bob has noticed times when it's *less* likely. It
largely comes down to the fact that it's not easy for a
three- to five-ton orca to haul its body out of the water.
For a human analogy, think about spending 20 minutes
doing jumping jacks versus going for a walk. The jumping jacks would be more tiring, wouldn't they? Similarly,
for orcas, breaching requires more energy than just
swimming along.

Now think about doing those jumping jacks when
you haven't eaten all day. Bob found orcas do fewer
breaches and fin- and tail-slaps when salmon are scarce.
That's probably because hungry whales have less energy.

Playtime at Sea

When Cookie was about six months old, Cindy Hansen, the education coordinator at Orca Network, was watching his family resting near San Juan Island.

"Once they all woke up, they headed out to go feeding," she recalls. "Everyone else was swimming, and Cookie was breaching the whole way. It reminded me of a little kid who's holding onto their mom's hand, but instead of walking, they're skipping. He was so cute."

Young Cookie breaches from the water. *Cindy Hansen*

They may also need to focus their time and attention on getting food and postpone the fun and games.

~~~~~~~

There are many more intriguing orca behaviors for scientists and curious kids to examine. The Center for Whale Research has a list that includes back dives and belly flops, lunges and half-breaches, burps and cartwheels.

And then there's another one of my favorites: the spyhop.

When orcas come up to breathe, they usually expose just the top of their head and blowhole. But when an orca spyhops, it sticks its whole head out of the water,

Onyx spyhops. *Danielle Carter*

sometimes far enough to show its fins. The movement looks graceful, a smooth rise and fall that lasts only a moment.

"There's something so delightful about whales that are traveling horizontally, and then they just poke their heads straight up," says research assistant Kate Laboda with a grin.

Other kinds of whales and dolphins spyhop too. Many scientists think it's because they want to peek above the surface and see what's around. But nobody knows for sure.

Bob and his team are fine with that.

"As much as we're in here being scientists, there's a part of me that wonders if I really need to know everything about these whales to appreciate them and want to fight for them," says Stephanie.

"Being a scientist is fun," Bob adds. "Just when you think you have a good understanding of what these whales are doing, they change. One time, J pod came by and went in a circle right in front of us and then kept going. You just put your pencil down and think, *Why did they just do that?*"

The Southern Resident orcas are the most-studied whales in the world, and researchers are learning fascinating things. But these orcas are still full of mysteries. While we may never unlock them all, it's fun to try.

The Kelping Game

Orcas like to swim through beds of kelp—large brown towering algae—in play. They drape slippery kelp blades over their dorsal fins or tails, drag the kelp blades with their mouths, or push them around with their heads. I imagine it being similar to humans dressing up or balancing bean bags on our heads for a field day race.

Mega demonstrates "kelping." Taken under NMFS permit 781-1824/16163. *Candice Emmons*

Where Giants Can Still Disappear

Crossing my fingers for a day with orcas, I hopped into a small boat with the team from Soundwatch, a Whale Museum program that has been educating boaters for nearly three decades. Leaving the harbor behind, we headed out into the open water between San Juan Island and Victoria, British Columbia. It was summer, but the wind was freezing. I put on a second coat and shivered with a mixture of cold and anticipation. Even though I was tagging along with experts, there was no guarantee we'd find orcas.

Given their enormity—an adult male Southern Resident may be 26 feet long (8 m) and weigh as much as a school bus full of kids—it seems like they should be easy to spot. But they're only visible to us humans when they come up to breathe or breach or spyhop. Those moments total just 5 percent of an orca's day.

The Soundwatch team also couldn't be sure the orcas were here in the inland waters of the Salish Sea. One day, the orcas can be tracked by whale-watching boats or researchers collecting data. Then the next morning, nobody has any idea where the orcas are. The three pods spread out across hundreds of miles as they roam in search of salmon, traveling up to 75 miles (120 km) in a day. They go north to British Columbia and southeast to Alaska. They swim down to the mouth of the Columbia River on the border between Washington and Oregon. And sometimes they venture even farther south. In 2019, they were spotted in Monterey Bay, California, the first confirmed sighting there in eight years.

The Soundwatch coordinator cut our boat's engine, and we scanned the horizon. No dorsal fins in sight. On the radio, whale-watching captains exchanged messages, and it was clear everyone was searching and waiting, just like us.

On average, orcas swim about 8 miles per hour (13kph), or a 7.5-minute mile; maybe you could run that fast on shore. But when they want to—like when chasing something scrumptious—they can nearly quadruple that speed, accelerating to 30 miles per hour (50 kph).

No orcas appeared that morning, so we followed a pair of humpbacks traveling north and stopped to talk to recreational boaters about responsible whale-watching.

I really wanted to see an orca. But I also found it magical that these huge animals can vanish overnight. With all the technology and satellites in use today, it seems like we can track anything on Earth. But the orcas still evade our attempts for days and weeks on end.

Sometimes, that makes it harder for us to help them. Scientists need to find the orcas in order to study them and learn what's threatening their recovery. Ship captains need to know if whales are nearby so they can avoid hitting them. In the case of sick orca Scarlet, researchers and veterinarians wanted to find her to check on how she was doing and try to give her medicine.

To me, it feels like the balance is just about right, for now: Many days pass when the orcas can vanish and be wild, hopefully roaming quieter waters without as much disturbance from humans. But then they are spotted again and people—filled with excitement and wonder—can witness their magic, study what's wrong, or do something to protect them.

Government scientists used to put tracking tags on the dorsal fins of some Southern Resident orcas. The tags had satellite transmitters and helped the scientists study where they went. But that changed in 2016, when they tagged Nigel (L95), a 20-year-old orca from L pod.

The first effort to tag Nigel didn't work. The tag fell into the sea. Before reattaching it to Nigel, the scientists

Swim Season

From spring to fall, the Southern Residents have typically spent much of their time in the inland waters of the Salish Sea.

In the winter, they tend to be along the outer coast. It's particularly hard for scientists to find and study orcas out there in the open ocean, where the waves are big and little research boats can't get the job done.

Those travel patterns reflect where the orcas have historically found salmon at different times of year. But whales aren't on a strict schedule, and they can't count on finding salmon where they used to. This means they can be anywhere in their range at any time. We can never be sure when and where these whales will pop up next.

disinfected the tag, but perhaps not well enough. Nigel got a fungal infection that likely entered his bloodstream through the wound where the tracking tag was attached. He died five weeks after the tagging.

Upon close inspection after his death, experts agreed that while Nigel had other health issues and wasn't getting enough to eat, the fungal infection directly contributed to his death. The government stopped tagging Southern Residents indefinitely, even though they had put similar tags on seven other orcas in the past without any apparent harm. On such a small, vulnerable population, it was just too risky.

～～～～～

An organization called Orca Network gathers information in another way, at least when the orcas are in the inland waters of Washington state: they collect reports from people who have spotted whales from shore or from boats and immediately share those sightings in ways that can help.

"We alert people to 'Be Whale Wise,'" says Cindy Hansen, Orca Network's education and advocacy coordinator, referring to the rules and regulations for boats near whales. "We also let ferry captains know when orcas are going to be in the ferry lanes, so they watch for them and slow down." And they alert researchers so they can get out right away on boats or along the shore to collect data.

Perhaps most importantly, the sighting information is available to the public on the Orca Network Facebook page.

"It's a way of helping connect people with the whales, if they can get out and watch them from shore," Cindy says. "Then they want to learn more—and want to protect them."

People get a close-up view of the orcas from Point Robinson in Washington State. *Jim Diers*

One fall morning, sitting at my desk, I took a break from writing and scanned the Orca Network page. A recent post made me sit up straighter: "10:50: Orcas moving south into Rich Passage."

That's not far from here, I thought. *It's already been 20 minutes since that post went up, but maybe it's not too late to see them.* These weren't the endangered Southern Residents, but the chance to see any whales always gets my heart rate up. I texted my husband, Stuart, who'd taken our only car to visit family: "There's orca action off the south end of Bainbridge Island." He responded to say he'd be home soon. I wondered how soon.

On the Lookout

Cindy Hansen has felt a connection to whales since she was little, initially inspired by a book. As she went through middle school and high school, she found she loved acting and debating. That pointed her to a career in public speaking and education. With those skills, she's playing an important role in the human superpod that's helping the orcas, reaching out to many other people and inspiring them to take action.

"I've talked to a lot of people who have this kind of passion for whales," Cindy tells me. "They say the same thing—it's something you can't describe; it's just something that's there, as you probably know well."

I nod. My fascination with whales feels like it's rooted deep in my soul.

All around the Salish Sea, people are always on the lookout for orcas. And the orcas' ability to seemingly vanish—or suddenly appear—only adds to the excitement of spotting them amid the waves.

(continued on the next page)

"It's hilarious. How do 20 animals just disappear?" asks Cindy. "I actually love it when that happens. The sightings are important, and they're great to help connect people to the whales, but I still think it's funny that they have the ability to disappear with so many eyes on them. It just shows that even with all our scientific advances, they're still the ones in charge."

A few minutes later, a new post appeared on the Orca Network page: "11:25: They're off Lytle Beach near the red buoy, milling around."

Lytle Beach is a 10-minute drive away! What if I miss them? Hands shaking, I sent a new message, making it crystal clear I needed Stuart to bring the car home immediately.

Seconds later, I heard the garage door open. He knows me well. I grabbed my coat and jumped in the car.

As Stuart drove, I checked my phone. New posts said the orcas swam east, so we turned down a road that led to a park. We got out and immediately spotted black dorsal fins in the distance. We ran half a mile along the shore and stopped near a dozen other people focused on the same thing: five orcas, right in front of us.

The orcas got my full attention—all the usual distractions, from cell phone buzzes to hunger pangs, didn't stand a chance against the magnificence of these crea-tures and the anticipation of where they might come up next. I watched their dorsal fins emerge, heading one way and then another as they circled for a magical half-hour. Gradually, they continued around the point until they were out of sight. I liked thinking about other people who had seen the Orca Network posts and were eagerly gathering on shorelines to the north, waiting for those five whales to appear.

We need to learn more about the Southern Residents to better protect them; finding them is part of that work.

Scarlet approaches eager onlookers near Lime Kiln Light-house. Taken under NMFS permit 18786. *Katy Foster/NOAA Fisheries*

And if people know where the orcas are, they can help keep them safe amid busy boat traffic and spread the word so others can see them from shore and be inspired to help these whales.

But I also believe there can be safety—and magic—in these enormous animals slipping away from our technology, noise, and boats, and I hope we'll all give them plenty of chances to do that.

Why Are Other Orcas Doing Better?

In September 2020, wildfires burned across the western United States. I'd followed the health warnings and taken refuge inside, away from the smoke. Occasionally, I glanced out the window at the sea, though I could only see a few hundred yards. Everything glowed in eerie yellowish gray as the sun fought to get through.

Then I spotted three orcas in the haze. If anything was going to make me brave the choking smoke, it was the chance to watch whales. I grabbed a face mask to breathe easier and ran outside.

The three orcas weren't traveling steadily north or south but staying in one area, pointing in a new direction each time they came up. They were hunting.

I knew a trio was a sign they were unlikely to be Southern Residents, who typically travel in larger family groups. A group of only three orcas could be stealthy and listen for their prey's vocalizations or splashes.

Soon after, I glimpsed their target: a harbor seal, poking its head up for a breath of air.

The seal dove under, and the three orcas converged a moment later in that spot with a great splash. I thought they must have caught the seal, but a few minutes later it emerged again near a bed of kelp. Methodically, the orcas chased it down the shore, trying to ram it or corner it in a cove, sometimes lunging so close to the rocks I thought they would crash. The seal must have been getting tired, but unlike the giant orcas, it was small and nimble and could change direction quickly underwater.

The chase lasted for well over an hour, as suspenseful as any action movie. I ran down the shore to keep up until I faced a wide crevice in the rocks, the cliff plunging down to crashing waves below. I considered scrambling around but knew it'd take way too long. The orcas were moving fast, still in hot pursuit. Pinning my binoculars on them, I watched through the smoke until they were out of sight. As I went back inside, I wondered if the seal would manage to get away.

~~~~~~

The transient orcas I spotted—also called Bigg's killer whales after researcher Dr. Mike Bigg—are hanging out in the Salish Sea more and more. In the 1970s, Mike and his colleagues thought these orcas were social outcasts who couldn't fit in with Southern Resident pods. But Mike, Dr. John Ford, and other scientists took a closer look and discovered the transients and the Southern Residents frequent some of the same waters but are completely different.

Transients look very similar to the Southern Residents, but if you examine pictures closely, you can see they have chunkier dorsal fins and more nicks and scratches. Unlike the Southern Residents, they don't stay in stable family groups for life. They don't interbreed with the Southern Residents—and DNA shows they haven't for many thousands of years—and they don't

A transient orca flings a sea lion pelt after a successful hunt.
Danielle Carter

make any of the same calls. Genetically, the transients are actually more closely related to orcas in the Atlantic Ocean than they are to the Southern Residents. And the Southern Residents and the transients typically steer clear of each other.

Also, transients are thriving, their population now more than four times larger than the Southern Resident population. Why is that?

The evidence was right in front of me on that smoky day: the transients have a completely different menu. Whereas the Southern Residents eat only fish, the transients hunt marine mammals—not fish.

For years, human hunters decimated seal and sea lion populations. Those must have been tough times for the transient orcas. Then, after Congress passed the Marine Mammal Protection Act in 1972, seal and sea lion numbers began to rebound dramatically. Today, coastal areas are like an all-you-can-eat-buffet for the transient orcas.

Though as I observed, the transient orcas still have to work for their meals. They must stay silent, listening carefully to find their prey. The *click-click-click* from an echolocation search, as well as any chattering back and forth to each other, would mean game over. Salmon can't hear orca calls and clicks, but marine mammals can. And they'd know just what to do: get the heck out of there!

When these orcas identify a target, they may spend a couple of hours working together to weaken it before they can grab on. They ram into their prey, strike it with their tails, block its shore escape, and drown it. Some scientists think transients might break even their silence to scream, scaring the animal into a bay where it'll be easier to trap.

Luckily for the transients, if a seal does manage to slip away from their grasp, there's probably another just around the bend. Meanwhile, the Southern Residents are finding their usual foraging hotspots are like restaurants that have run out of the only thing they can eat.

While orca populations around the world eat everything from fish to seals to sharks to other whales, each individual population focuses on a small subset of those options. As specialists, they are more efficient at foraging. They fine-tune the skills needed to catch one kind of food and build up an intimate knowledge of where and how to find it. Those skills rarely transfer well to other kinds of food.

For example, Southern Residents specialize in hunting salmon. They are really good at finding and catching salmon because they remember where salmon return to rivers in different seasons. They call to each other to share information when they spot salmon. And they have a lot of practice hunting independently, using echolocation to zero in on a fish and chasing it until they can grab it with their teeth.

Transients, on the other hand, don't need to go to different parts of the ocean at the right times of year, because seals and sea lions can be anywhere, year-round. They can't afford to scare off tasty marine mammals by traveling in big groups, calling to each other, or having exuberant superpod splash parties. They've learned to be stealthy and to work strategically in small teams to bring down their prey.

Southern Residents' salmon-hunting instincts would make it nearly impossible for them to catch large mammals like seals or porpoises. Scientists also don't believe the Southern Residents will try. That's because orcas learn what food is from infancy, when their family members share what they catch with them. Nothing but fish will ever look like food to a Southern Resident.

"They can't change their diet," says Dr. Deborah Giles, a scientist at Wild Orca (who goes by her last name). "They have this deep, intense cultural direction from their moms to *not eat that [other] thing.*"

Unfortunately, with all the changes brought by humans, salmon are scarce. The Southern Residents' narrow specialization is no longer beneficial. Today, it's hurting their chance of survival.

The Canine in the Superpod

Eba stands alert at the front of the small motorboat, buckled into a life jacket, focusing on her job—a job only a talented and well-trained dog can do. She sniffs out whale poop (scat) floating on the ocean waves from up to a mile away.

Eba is a mixed-breed dog and the companion and colleague of Dr. Giles at Wild Orca. They're practically celebrities in the human—and now canine—superpod working to help the orcas. I'm excited to be riding on the boat with this duo, as well as Giles's husband Jim Rappold, the vessel captain, and Minola Motha de Silva, a college intern.

A few minutes after leaving the dock, Giles points over the side of the boat and explains that first, we look

Eba focuses on sniffing out orca scat. *Nora Nickum*

at the "background" of the water. That means checking out what's floating around in the sea, so we don't get distracted by fluff or seaweed or other things later in the search for the real prize: orca poop. The water is fairly clear, with some seeds and a bunch of tiny flies scattered on top. The sea is also calm, which is good news for me—I forgot to bring any seasickness medication. More importantly, calm water is good news for Giles and Eba in their quest for scat. And there's just a slight breeze.

"We can't have *no* wind; those are frustrating days," Giles explains; there has to be enough wind to carry the scent to Eba. "We can't have days that are *too* windy. And we can't have the tides shifting so fast that the samples are whipped out of range before we can turn and get them."

The endangered Southern Residents aren't in the area, so we're after transient orca scat. Jim maneuvers the boat until three orcas are several hundred yards ahead of us—visible, but certainly not close. We can see their dorsal fins emerging and misty breath from their blowholes.

Dr. Sam Wasser from the University of Washington came up with the idea of using scat detection dogs to do noninvasive research on endangered animals like the orcas back in 1997. He started the Conservation Canines program. Giles was initially a vessel captain for that program before working at the front of the boat with Eba.

Hands-off, "noninvasive" research like this is important, Giles tells me. "We want to try to eliminate any potential for our boat to be a stressful situation for the whales. We use a dog because it allows us to be so much farther away. We can be a quarter mile away, easily, and still sample that area behind the whales."

Eba rides at the front of the boat. She's working hard already. As soon as a whale poops, Eba will know. She can smell Southern Resident orca scat up to one nautical mile (1.8 km) away from where it's floating in the water. That's five times farther away than a human could see it, and *much* farther than a human could smell it.

But the team has been out in the boat trailing behind transient orcas for at least 15 days this summer with no luck, so getting samples isn't guaranteed.

Suddenly, Eba starts wagging her tail. She puts her front paws up on the edge of the boat. Those are signs that one of the whales pooped, and Eba has gotten a faint whiff of that scat.

Orca scat must be collected quickly. Giles and Eba usually only have several minutes—no more than half an hour—before the scat sinks. And it's not easy to locate, even after Eba signals there's a sample out there. The water moves, the boat moves, the wind changes. Eba must keep working hard to track the scent and point Giles in the right direction. If they pass the strongest scent, Eba will come back along the side of the boat, trying to run back to it.

"That's when I know to turn into the wind," Giles has explained to me. "I tell the driver to follow Eba's nose. Literally where her nose is pointing, that's where we take the boat."

Giles watches Eba closely and points to show Jim, at the wheel, which direction Eba is leading us. Eba licks her lips and leans over the edge a bit, pulling on her leash.

I peer at the water but see nothing resembling orca poop—not that I really know what I'm looking for. But expert Giles, with a higher viewpoint at the bow of the boat, sees something and calls out.

Jim quickly tosses a handful of cereal toward the spot Giles and Eba are pointing at. Without a floating marker like that, it would be really hard to locate the spot where they thought they'd seen something.

He circles the boat back around as we all scan the water near the cereal, looking for something that might be orca poop. Giles spots it first—kind of a curled worm shape, floating just under the surface—and scoops it up with a beaker at the end of a long pole. We all clap and cheer. Giles immediately passes the beaker to Eba to reinforce the scent and tie it to the pending reward. Eba whimpers and bounces with intense excitement.

Why is Eba so excited about poop? She anticipates an immediate reward for a job well done: a few minutes of playtime with her favorite toy in the world, a knotted rope.

Minola starts playing a vigorous game of tug-of-war with a clearly ecstatic Eba, while Giles scoops two more scat samples from the water.

Giles checks to see if she managed to scoop up any traces of orca scat. *Nora Nickum*

Giles asks if I want to smell one, and I nod eagerly—Eba's excitement was contagious. I put my nose right up to the beaker and sniff. Given that the whale was definitely not a vegetarian, I'm surprised to catch a scent like alfalfa. The scat looks like an extra-hairy pipe cleaner, with remnants of fur from a marine mammal. Considering the size of the whale that left it behind, the scat is remarkably tiny, only a couple of inches long. Maybe there was more that sank before we found it.

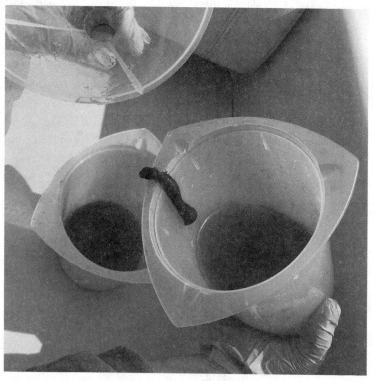

This transient orca poop, though tiny, will help scientists learn a ton. *Nora Nickum*

Giles tells me Southern Resident poop, in contrast, is more likely to smell like slightly old fish, which essentially it is, and look like a splotch of messy pancake batter.

She begins processing the samples right there in the boat, pouring off the extra water and putting the remaining material in small tubes. When she returns to shore, she'll put the scat samples into a freezer until they can be processed by technicians and graduate students in the lab at the University of Washington.

"We have to wait until we have enough samples to outfit the lab to be able to run all of them at the same time," Giles says. It may be fall or early next year before she gets the results from this summer's samples.

～～～～～

Because an animal's diet affects the smell of its scat, dogs must be specifically trained to find scat from particular species. Eba doesn't have as much practice sniffing out transient orca scat as Southern Resident scat, so Giles, Jim, and Minola are thrilled she found one today. They're also glad to get a sample that is large enough to use a bit of it for Eba's training sessions.

Giles notes that the best scat detection dogs are highstrung. Some were left at shelters; their original human families must have decided they were difficult pets. But the same characteristics make these dogs perfect for the scat-detection job. Because they would rather play than eat, they have a strong incentive to work hard—

finding scat—for that chance to play. Work hard, play hard.

Giles adopted Eba from her sister, who was fostering Eba after she was found abandoned outside a California animal shelter. Giles didn't initially intend to train Eba for scat detection. She had Eba for two years before giving that a try.

"One of our former trainers, Heath, was here visiting," recounts Giles. "I was standing there talking with him, and the whole time, Eba was shoving her toy into his hand. I wasn't paying much attention, just kind of concerned that she was being irritating or something, but at one point he stopped and said, 'Have you ever thought of training her to be a scent dog? Do you want

Minola rewards Eba with playtime. *Nora Nickum*

me to test her? Give her the first go-around that I'd give any dog we were considering?'"

Giles says she eagerly agreed. "He took her rope toy, rubbed it under his armpits and in his hair and stank it up a bit, and tossed it into waist-high grass. Without a thought, Eba bounded into the grass and got it."

Heath turned to Giles and said, "Yeah, she could definitely be trained."

The senior trainers from Conservation Canines joined Giles and Eba the following summer to start work, but Eba only needed a few days of training. After practicing finding scat under rocks and in holes on land, they waited for the whales to return. On her second day on the boat, Eba found her first whale scat by herself.

Giles still remembers the day. "July 6, 2019, was her very first sample," she tells me proudly. Since then, Eba has found over 80 more Southern Resident orca scat samples.

The training is ongoing, but Eba won't forget how to find scat samples. "It's about keeping us humans trained," says Giles. "It's about making sure we know how to read her."

Eba is six years old at the time of writing, and Giles predicts she probably has another six years of work in her. Then Eba will get to retire and spend her days relaxing at home.

Who's Who?

Sometimes Giles is pretty sure which orca left the scat, but it can be tricky when she and Eba are following a large group of whales. There are DNA records for nearly every Southern Resident orca, so Giles and her team compare the DNA in the scat sample to a DNA catalog and look for a match.

Scientists also use the DNA catalog to sort out orca family trees. While it's easy to tell who a calf's mother is because they stick close together, that's not the case for the father. DNA tests can pinpoint paternity right away.

When Eba successfully finds an orca scat, "it's a wonderful, frenetic time," Giles says, which I'm thrilled to get to witness on the boat. Finding scat is exciting for Eba because it means playtime, but it's also exciting for Giles, particularly when it comes to Southern Resident orcas. For one thing, it means the endangered whales are finding plenty of food.

"Sometimes they aren't pooping because they haven't had enough to eat the day before," Giles explains. "They need to be eating 300 to 450 pounds of food per day per whale on average to be giving up samples that we're able to collect."

Giles and her colleagues have even made tongue-in-cheek "Everybody Loves a Pooping Whale" bumper stickers. They highlight the importance of making sure the endangered orcas have enough salmon to eat, and also that studying scat reveals important clues about orcas' diets, stress levels, health, and genetics.

"One scat sample is like a gold mine. We can mine it for so much information," Giles says. "We're able to understand so much more about what is happening with that individual whale and extrapolate to what is happening to its family and pod."

With a tiny sample—less than one-quarter teaspoon (0.5–1 mL)—Giles's colleagues in the lab can look at hormones that tell them about the orca's stress level, nutrition, and pregnancy status. With a bigger sample, they can look for toxicants (PCBs, DDT, PBDEs) that have washed into the ocean and been taken up by fish—and then by the whale that ate those fish.

The results tell Giles so much about that individual whale. She'll know if it was having a hard time getting food because of more noise, and if it was stressed out from hunger. She can also learn about the amount of toxic chemicals circulating in the whale's body and if there were any parasites, fungus, or bacteria that could be making the animal sick.

Giles also studies the hormones in the scat samples to learn when whales are pregnant. Unfortunately, this research has shown that 69 percent of Southern Resident orca pregnancies detected over a six-year period were unsuccessful. The scat samples indicated females were pregnant, but later, when those whales should have been seen with calves, there were no youngsters in sight. That means the mother whales lost the pregnancies or their calves died right after birth. The primary reason appears to be not enough food—Chinook salmon—followed by a release of toxicants from their blubber when they don't get enough to eat.

Giles's findings point to things that elected officials, government agencies, and the public can and should do to help these whales, starting with increasing the number of salmon available for them to eat.

~~~~~~

While I'm out on the boat with Giles and Eba, people on shore—including my husband and young daughter—are getting much closer views of the transient orcas than we are. Giles always tries to stay far enough away from the whales that the boat doesn't disturb them.

As we motor back north along the shore of San Juan Island, Giles points out the outcropping at the county park where she first saw the Southern Residents. She was 18, and it was the moment that jump-started her passion for these whales and her life's work. Today, she's using her scientific training to do everything she can to help them.

"I see them as a better version of us. Their tight bonds, and the way they express those social bonds, like caring for each other when they're ill. Their sense of family. Foraging with and for each other when they are healthy and when they're hungry. They give us humans something to strive for."

The Bad Stuff

There are several toxic chemicals of concern for orcas and people:

- ⊘ PCBs were used to make things like paints, plastics, and electrical equipment. They weaken immune systems, increase cancer risk, and make it harder to have babies.

- ⊘ DDT was used to kill insects that people considered pests. DDT affects animals' ability to have babies.

- ⊘ PBDEs prevent clothing, rugs, and cars from catching on fire. But studies show PBDEs affect animals' brain development and livers.

(continued on the next page)

Some of these chemicals were banned decades ago, but they're still out there in the environment. PCBs, for example, won't drop to safe levels for most of the Southern Resident population until 2090. You'll have finished school, had jobs, and be past retirement age by then! Meanwhile, new pollution flows into the ocean whenever rain washes chemicals off roads and industrial lots.

The chemicals get locked up in an orca's blubber, but only until the orca needs to draw on that blubber for energy or to make milk for her calf. The firstborn calf in particular takes in a lot of its mother's lifetime buildup of bad chemicals.

Finding Friends

Tofino (J56) and Kiki (J53), two young female orcas, are close. And while we know family bonds are important to the Southern Residents, Tofino and Kiki don't have the same mom.

The relationship seemed to start with Kiki, age three, babysitting newborn Tofino in 2019. A few years later, they're still hanging out and playing. When they travel, they swim right up against each other, touching almost the whole time. Meanwhile, Tofino still benefits sometimes from the care of loving babysitters, including young females Star (J46) and Suttles (J40), who also aren't closely related to Tofino but take good care of her.

These close relationships outside the immediate family were a relatively recent discovery.

"The family structure is of course really, really important," says Dr. Michael Weiss from the Center for Whale Research. "It's still the most important thing in killer whale life. But there's richness in their social structure beyond that."

A few years ago, Michael flew a drone over J pod to get a bird's-eye view of their underwater activity, revealing behaviors that can't be seen from land or a boat. The most surprising discovery: orcas make close friends and babysit calves besides just their younger brothers and sisters.

Kiki (bottom) and Tofino (top) chase a salmon. Taken under NMFS permit 21238. *Center for Whale Research/University of Exeter*

Michael recalls watching Tofino and Kiki chasing a fish. Tofino was going after it and not having a lot of luck, even with Kiki's apparent efforts to help.

"The fish got away, and as they swam away together, they were contacting each other a little bit," Michael says. "It almost seemed like, 'It's all right, we'll get it next time.' They're really sweet."

He's particularly fond of Tofino, so seeing her hanging out with pal Kiki and building other strong relationships makes him happy: "Oh, you're making friends, you're getting a good social circle. Good for you!"

And it *is* good—social bonds help orcas survive. If Tofino has lots of friends who catch fish, she can eat more often. She might also get more information about where to find fish herself—beyond what she'll learn from her mom—as she hangs out with friends and goes to places where they've found food recently.

~~~~~~

I've spent countless hours watching the orcas from shore, but the view from the air is completely different—and moving. When I check out Michael's aerial videos and photos, I see orcas swimming side by side and coming up for air at the same time. It reminds me of close friends walking down the hallway together at school. And the emotional connection between the orcas feels even more palpable as they get close and rub their backs together. Michael says physical touch is important for bonding in a lot of mammals, and orcas are no exception.

From the video footage, Michael concluded the orcas typically make friends with others of the same sex and similar age. He goes through each video clip over and over, focusing on a different whale each time: "I say, OK, who did J51 [Nova] come into contact with? Who did he snuggle with?"

In Nova's case, the answer turned out to be T'ílem I'nges (J49), a young male also in J pod. Nova and T'ílem

The orcas hanging out together on the left are (bottom to top) Nova with mom Eclipse and T'ílem I'nges with mom Hy'Shqa. Another orca follows behind on the right. Taken under NMFS permit 21238. *Center for Whale Research/University of Exeter*

Why the Bite Marks?

Orcas often have rake marks on their bodies, made by the teeth of their fellow whales. Michael and his colleagues are studying drone footage to look for evidence of aggression among the Southern Residents. So far, they're finding combative behavior is very rare.

Could the rake marks happen during play, then? The team hopes to discover if orcas with more social connections also have more rake marks. If so, extra rake marks might be the badge of a particularly social whale.

I'nges aren't close relatives, but Michael documented them frequently hanging out and interacting. Orca best buds.

"Their moms are also pretty good friends," Michael says. That's Hy'Shqa and Eclipse. "They spend quite a bit of time together."

Nova and T'ílem I'nges are often joined by other young males: Mako, Notch, and Moby. "We see that group, and it's like, 'Oh yeah, it's the boys' club, here they are, they're doing their thing,'" Michael says with a grin.

Youngsters like these have plenty of time to hang out because they can rely on their grandmas and other grownups to help them get food. Hunting salmon isn't a full-time job just yet. Like young humans, they focus on learning, playing, and building friendships that feel like they'll last forever.

An Ocean Full of Noise

What's it like to search for fish in a vast, dark sea? Humans rely heavily on our sense of sight, so we'd struggle to find food in that environment. Orcas, on the other hand, evolved to depend on a different sense: sound.

Similar to a bat, an orca echolocates, sending out sound waves we can hear as a mechanical *click-click-click*. The sound waves bounce off things and return to the orca, traveling through a fatty part of its lower jaw and from there to the ear and brain. The information in the echo tells the orca what it found in the darkness. When researchers hear slow, occasional clicks over the hydrophones, it likely means the orca is finding its way, keeping track of other whales or boats. When the clicks speed up—to as many as 200 per second—it's zeroing in on something, such as a tasty-sounding fish.

That system worked superbly for orcas for thousands of years—until humans changed their underwater world. We've added our own clicks, bangs, whirs, rumbles, clatters, and pings to the ocean. Cities pound pilings into the seafloor to build ports and piers. Companies drill for oil.

Fishy Sounds

Salmon have a swim bladder like a balloon to help them adjust their depth in the water. That swim bladder, which reflects orcas' sound waves quite well, varies in shape and position from one salmon species to another. So an orca knows if it's after a Chinook just from the information carried by that echo.

Scientists don't think salmon can hear or sense an orca's echolocation clicks. But an approaching orca moves the water around it. When a salmon feels that difference in water pressure through what's known as the lateral line that runs along its side, it'll flee. The orca, in hot pursuit, sends out a steady stream of clicks, so it doesn't lose track of the fish—and can hopefully nab it.

Container ships with loud propellers and engines bring us things we ordered online. Fishing boats use sonar signals to find fish. The navy tests sonar equipment. People zip around in motorboats or travel on ferries. It's hard for an orca to hear its own echoing clicks amid all that noise. And that means it's hard for them to find food—especially now that salmon are scarce.

Imagine you're in a grocery store, hungry for lunch, when the power goes out. You can hardly see. And the shelves are mostly bare. Like an orca in a noisy sea, you'd spend a lot of time and energy getting a meal and probably feel pretty stressed out.

Underwater noise doesn't just get in the way of orcas eating—it also affects their ability to communicate with each other. This time, imagine you're in a really loud cafeteria, trying to talk to your friend at the far end of the table. You'd need to speak up, maybe even shout. That would take more energy, wouldn't it? Scientists are learning orcas do the same. They call more loudly when their environment is noisy, and that costs them energy. The orcas have also lengthened the duration of their calls over time and in the presence of more boats, which may be another effort to be heard through the noise. Imagine instead of saying "Over here!" you're always having to shout "OOOOOOOVER HEEEEEERE!"

With ports and big cities like Seattle and Vancouver right on the Salish Sea, there's constant, loud traffic from container ships and tankers, motorboats, and ferries transporting passengers from islands to the mainland

People watch an L pod orca named Surprise! (L86) from a boat in 2010, before distance guidelines changed. Taken under NMFS permit 718-1824/16163. *Brad Hanson/NWFSC*

and back. And during my summer visits to San Juan Island, I'm more likely to notice the arrival of orcas not because of the *pfewww* from their blowholes, but because I hear the rumble of engines from accompanying recreational and whale-watching boats.

The first commercial tours focused on orcas began in British Columbia in 1980. By 2019, there were dozens of US and Canadian whale-watching companies offering trips in the San Juan Islands and surrounding areas. Private boaters and kayakers also stop to watch whales. The Whale Museum's Soundwatch Boater Education team counted as many as 35 boats with transient or Southern Resident orcas at one time in the summer of 2021. In the prior decade it had been as high as 80 boats.

Over half a million people go whale-watching on commercial or private boats in Washington and British Columbia every year. And the popularity of that activity has its pros and cons. On the one hand, that's a lot of people to rally to the cause of saving these whales. Seeing orcas can inspire people to care and take action to protect them. The whale-watching industry is also important because it supports a lot of jobs.

On the other hand, nearby vessels of any kind can hinder orcas' feeding. That's a particular concern when salmon are in short supply, and the orcas are hungry. Studies show orcas spend less time foraging for food and more time traveling when there are boats within 400 yards (360 m). If boaters slow down, that reduces noise. But even quiet boats like kayaks, or motorboats or ferries with their engines off, have an impact. Orcas need to surface for air, and boats are obstacles they have to pay attention to and maneuver around. That means they can't fully concentrate on finding and catching fish.

The Southern Residents need more space and quiet. Scientists are continuing to examine the specific effects of noise and boat presence, which can help us target solutions.

~~~~~~~~

If you want to talk to an orca researcher, you have to be flexible. If the weather is good and the whales show up, the researcher is likely to have last-minute plans that matter more than any meeting on their calendar.

Dr. Marla Holt and I scheduled our conversation for a day when the weather forecast looked terrible: heavy rain. As predicted, she was land-bound. That was frustrating for her, amid her annual, narrow three-week window to do her orca studies, but good news for me.

Marla, a wildlife biologist with the US government's Northwest Fisheries Science Center, studies how boats affect Southern Resident communication and behavior. Earlier that week, she and her team had been out on an inflatable research boat attaching electronic recording tags to orcas' backs.

Putting a temporary tag on Surprise! Taken under NMFS permit 16163. *Deborah Giles*

I ask how in the world one goes about sticking a cell-phone-sized device with a foot-long antenna onto the back of a moving orca.

Marla smiles. "It's incredibly challenging."

In the past, they tried using a device with a canister of air to launch the tag out toward the whale. That didn't work very well. Now, they use a long, lightweight pole. That works better, Marla says, but takes a lot of patience.

"When they are doing slow swimming, mellow behavior, we start to drive the boat at the same speed as the whales and get them used to us," she says. "Hopefully they start to forget we're there."

At that point, she tells me, researcher Jeff Hogan would be standing at the very front of the boat. He would lean over with the pole, watching for the second when an orca would come up for air, and quickly stick the tag on its back with suction cups.

I wonder what the orca thinks about that. Marla says usually orcas don't seem to react at all. Sometimes they flinch and dive down quickly but return to normal behavior within a few minutes.

These tags are safer than the tiny, darted satellite tags that pierce through a dorsal fin, which led to the deadly infection on Nigel several years ago. Those darted satellite tags stay on for a few weeks and only measure an orca's location. In contrast, Marla's suction-cup tags typically stay on for one day and measure everything from sound and temperature to pressure and magnetic forces. That gives scientists a way to observe in great detail what the orcas are doing and experiencing underwater.

Once the tag is attached, the team follows at a distance, watching closely to see if the tagged orca surfaces with a salmon. Later, they'll match the time the orca caught that fish to the tag data revealing all the sound and movement cues that happened underwater before the whale surfaced with its catch.

All the important data is stored on the tag, so getting it back is essential. Marla programs it to release at a certain time; an electrical signal corrodes a wire and releases the suction cups. Marla uses a big antenna to try to pick up the beeps from the tag's beacon and zero in on where it is.

In past years, the timer was usually set for just before sunset, so the team could see the tag floating on the water, grab it, and get back to land before dark. These days, Marla programs tags to stay on overnight, hoping to learn how much orcas are eating in the day versus at night. The team can't follow a tagged orca in the dark, so they come back the next day. It's much easier to find a whale than a tiny tag on its own, so they try to arrive before the tag falls off the orca.

But luck isn't always on their side. In 2020, they put an overnight tag on Rainshadow (K37), a 16-year-old orca. They found him the next morning, but with no tag on his back. A frantic search began, like a high-stakes treasure hunt.

A tag costs thousands of dollars. To save money, the scientists rent the tags for just a few weeks each year. I imagine a scientist's anxiety over a lost tag being like that of a kid who begged Mom and Dad for a cell phone, *finally* got one—and then lost it.

With the whale tag, even more important than the money is the invaluable data it holds.

Marla on the research boat. *Isabelle Groc*

"It keeps you up at night." Marla grimaces.

They needed to find the tag quickly because the strong satellite signals beeping its location would stop when the battery connected to that component died, after about 48 hours. And the researchers had to be within a couple of kilometers to get a good signal. Complicating things further, the signal could get scrambled when it bounced off islands and cliffs. The tag would emit weaker radio signals too, but only for about a week. After that, the chance of finding a small tag floating in the ocean would be basically zero.

As the team searched for Rainshadow's dropped tag, thick wildfire smoke hung over the area, making it hard to see. Marla managed to pick up a signal about 24 hours after the tag disappeared. But currents and waves make a tag a moving target, and the location data Marla picked up was already several hours old.

Her team, along with research partners in Canada, tried everything they could think of. They climbed mountains to try to pick up radio signals. They carried tracking antennas on the local ferries. After a week of searching, they worried the signal was lost forever.

Then, as the smoke cleared, they went out in a research boat and detected a beep. They maneuvered until they found the tag and heaved a collective sigh of relief.

Every tag that is successfully put on an orca and found again provides a wealth of information into the orcas' hidden world, and Rainshadow's tag was no exception.

"The tags tell us what the whales are doing underwater," Marla says. "They have accelerometers like what we have in Fitbits or activity trackers, which know if you're moving, if you're doing aerobic exercise, if you're walking fast."

From the data, Marla can pinpoint shallow dives with slow, regular clicking. "We hear that when they're searching for prey, scanning their environment with a flashlight of sound."

Then there are the hunting dives. "When they've detected something or are in a place where they've found fish before, they dive deeper and start to produce faster clicks," Marla says. "And then when they get really close to yummy fish, they make really fast clicks that sound like a buzz to our ear. The whale is trying to keep that 'sound flashlight' in its acoustic field of view, kind of like how a cheetah would try to keep its eyes on a gazelle."

Next, Marla analyzes how many boats were around the tagged whale, how far away they were, and how fast they were going. She has learned that when boats are nearby, orcas make fewer dives that result in catching a fish. They also spend less time overall in what she calls "fish-catching behavior." But the biggest news from Marla's recent studies has been that female orcas are affected by boat traffic much more than males are. "Males did slightly different things if boats were close, but they were still foraging," Marla tells me. "With the females it was like, 'OK, I'm not going to forage anymore.'"

Marla thinks when mother orcas perceive vessels to be a risk, they choose to stay near their young ones and look out for them, rather than diving for food and leaving youngsters behind.

"Perhaps they're not comfortable with boats being that close," Marla says. "Or it might be related to having to keep track of close vessels. When they do deeper dives that involve catching fish, they're twisting and turning and changing direction and going up and down. They have to come up at some point to take a breath, and vessels at the surface might be an extra thing they have to pay attention to."

The effect on female orcas' behavior is worrisome because nursing mothers need to eat more. A calf's survival depends on having a healthy mother.

The boats likely also interfere with orcas' ability to share any fish they catch with their family members. That's something they do at the surface—where the boats are.

As you can see, ships, ferries, and even small boats and kayaks can cause several problems. They make orcas spend less time searching for and finding food. They make it harder for orcas to catch fish when they do find them. And they make orcas spend more energy while hunting and trying to communicate, so they ultimately need to eat more.

These challenges could be overcome if salmon were plentiful, but right now, that's not the case. We need to increase salmon abundance, and in the meantime, we need to reduce underwater noise to give orcas the best chance of finding food. And it turns out that to make things quiet, sometimes you have to speak up.

Quieting the Waters

In a formal, wood-paneled room draped with flags, I leaned into a microphone and took a deep breath. My policy job for the Seattle Aquarium had brought me to the Washington State Capitol. The members of a legislative committee sat in front of me. I needed to convince them the orcas needed more space and quiet on the water. These officials had the power to change the laws.

At that time, in early 2019, boaters had to stay just 200 yards (180 m) away from Southern Resident orcas. Even though faster boats are noisier, there was no speed limit. The orcas needed more protection.

"Reducing vessel noise and disturbance is something we can do *right now* that will have an immediate benefit for the orcas," I said.

HB 1580　ORCA WHALES/VESSELS　　　　　　　2/5/19
NORA NICKUM
SEATTLE AQUARIUM
HOUSE RURAL DEVELOPMENT, AGRICULTURE & NATURAL RESOURCES COMMITTEE

The author testifies in support of protections for orcas. *TVW*

The Washington State Legislature passed a new law as a result of many people speaking up. It required that all boats, motorized or not, be farther away from the endangered orcas than before: the length of three football fields instead of two. It also said boaters must slow to seven knots, or about eight miles per hour (13 km/hr), within a half nautical mile (0.9 km) of the orcas.

The state also required, for the first time, that whale-watching companies have licenses. The following year, I was part of a committee advising on rules for the license. Those rules ultimately limited the number of tours that could be near Southern Residents at one time. Operators can still take passengers to see other whales, like humpbacks and transient orcas, anytime. These changes, along with the ones that apply to all boaters, gave the orcas some more room and quieter waters to efficiently find and catch fish.

But just having a protective law isn't always enough. People also have to know what the law is and be willing to follow it. My joy in watching orcas from shore is always tinged with worry because I frequently see

Shhh . . .

We also need to reduce noise and disturbance from much larger boats. The Washington State Ferries, like the ones I ride to work in Seattle and the ones taking tourists to the San Juan Islands, are switching to hybrid-electric systems and slowing or stopping when whales are nearby. Meanwhile, many ship captains going to Vancouver, British Columbia, voluntarily slow down to reduce noise; captains heading to ports in Washington State are now being asked to do the same thing under a program called Quiet Sound. People are tackling this complex problem from all sides, trying to give these orcas a brighter future.

recreational boaters motor too close. Some seem to be angling for a closer view, while others just zip by, apparently oblivious to the enormous yet fragile creatures in their midst.

The Soundwatch team goes out on the water every day during the summer months to talk to boaters about how to keep orcas and other whales safe. Soundwatch recorded over 400 incidents in 2021, mostly recreational boaters going too fast around orcas or getting too close. Only half of the boaters they talked to knew the speed and distance rules. Can you imagine if only half of the drivers on the road knew the traffic laws? It's not possible to put up stop signs in the ocean; that's why it's so important for Soundwatch to visit docks and be out on the water, helping to ensure everyone hears about the rules.

I've seen Soundwatch teams, researchers, and whale-watching operators all wave flags or sound air horns when a private boater is heading straight into a pod of orcas. Some people stop when they see or hear the warnings. Others don't.

Fortunately, there's another member of the human superpod with the power to enforce the rules intended to keep orcas safe: a cop with a mission to protect animals.

~~~~~~~~

That cop is Taylor Kimball, and when he pops up on my computer screen for an interview, he's sitting in his truck, evergreen trees visible through his window.

"Looks like you're heading out," I say, and ask if we should reschedule for a time when he'll be at his office.

"This is my office," he says with a grin. "Actually, I do have an office, but I find I get more work done out of my truck. It's easier to listen to the radio and respond. If it's not the truck, it's the boat."

Taylor is a fish and wildlife enforcement officer. He's assigned to the area around the San Juan Islands because the orcas have typically spent a lot of time there. But when the orcas aren't around, he's still busy. He makes sure people aren't catching more salmon or shrimp than their license allows, rescues boaters in distress, and helps tow the occasional dead gray whale to shore.

Taylor tells me it's rare for him to have an agenda for the day that sticks. Urgent situations pop up all the time. A few days before we talked, for example, the whales hadn't been in town for a few days.

"And the weather the day before was really snotty," he says. Bad weather means boaters are unlikely to head out on the water for fun. So Taylor planned to do other work, unrelated to orcas. "Then I got a call from people on San Juan Island saying the Southern Residents had shown up that afternoon. I had to scramble and get out there on a boat."

Maybe you've seen drivers on the highway slow down when they realize a police car is following them or is parked in the median. The same thing happens on the water. If Taylor is on scene, there tend to be fewer violations. People know they can get in trouble.

"Often we'll run our blue lights when it starts to get crazy out there," Taylor says. "People stop and say, 'What's going on here that there are emergency lights on?' That's exactly what we want them to do. They look around and start pointing to whales. We've served the purpose of slowing them down, and they start following the rules."

Taylor can ticket boaters who get too close or go too fast around the whales. That could bring a fine of more than $1,000. But he feels like he's doing more to help the orcas when he talks to boaters about the plight of these endangered animals, and the rules. "Our number-one goal out on the water is education, hands down," he tells me. "We'll talk to them, let them know what the rules are."

He says when he does write a ticket, it's for someone who knows the rules—and doesn't care. "They're almost always repeat offenders. They go in and start breaking the rules again."

Taylor goes back and talks to them, giving them another chance, but even that's not always enough. If they break the rules yet again, Taylor has to change tactics if he's to keep the orcas safe. He drives the message home another way—with a ticket.

Ensuring all boaters know and follow the rules certainly helps protect the orcas. But even those law-abiding boats impact orcas' behavior and their ability to communicate and find scarce food. So, many people are choosing to watch orcas from land, instead.

~~~~~~~

I head to Alki Beach on a foggy October day. A faint smell of seaweed drifts past on the breeze, and I watch a baby gull pestering its mother for food.

All along the west coast of the United States, there are more than 130 Whale Trail sites where people have a good chance of seeing marine mammals like orcas from shore. This one is in the heart of Seattle. I spot the Space Needle poking up across the bay; downtown's skyscrapers are right around the corner.

Donna Sandstrom, founder of the Whale Trail, soon joins me. "We live on this urban fjord that hosts apex predators. That's rare, to have this close access to them."

Two people stand waist-deep in the frigid water below, chatting. Behind us, a group of people bursts into

People watch Hy'Shqa and Cookie from the beach at Point Robinson, on the Whale Trail. *Caroline Matter*

laughter, shedding layers and getting ready for their own cold-water plunge. A family walks by with a stroller.

"People used to be completely surprised to see orcas here, especially the Southern Residents," Donna says of the urban setting. "That's why I started the Whale Trail, because they've been here for tens of thousands of years. This is their home." She wanted people to know their underwater neighbors and launched the Whale Trail with a team of organizations that shared that vision.

Some visitors come to places like Alki with the hope of seeing orcas. Other people come across Whale Trail signs or the whales themselves unexpectedly while out walking or picnicking or riding a ferry.

Donna holds up a bag made from orca-print fabric. "We always bring down bags filled with binoculars. I love seeing the whales, but I love just as much helping other people have that experience."

We chat some more, and then she points past me. "We have some wildlife!" There's a shiny gray head bobbing in the waves—a harbor seal. As the most common marine mammal in the Salish Sea, harbor seals are easy to spot from most Whale Trail locations.

Today, there are no orcas in sight, but that's the thing about looking for whales from shore. It has an extra dose of unpredictability. You can't go to exactly where the whales are, like you could in a boat. But to me, it feels even luckier and more magical when I do get a close sighting from shore. And I don't worry about whether I'm getting in their way.

I ask Donna about times she's seen Southern Residents from where we're standing.

"I've actually seen J pod go right down Alki here, as close as that swimmer is." She points to someone less than 50 yards (46 m) away. "It's awesome."

Watching whales from shore, rather than from a boat, is a way to make the waters quieter for orcas, so they have a better chance of catching salmon. But whether people watch from land or boats or webcam, or listen via hydrophone, an orca sighting builds a personal connection to the orcas that inspires more people to join the human superpod and find their own way to help.

"When I say, 'We're watching J pod, they're one of our endangered Southern Resident pods,' the first thing people say is, 'How can I help; what can I do?'" Donna says, "Conservation starts with awareness and caring, and they're on board."

When Salmon Return

I stand on the banks of the Cedar River, which is swelling with last week's rain, and look down into the water. My eyes are first drawn to dozens of sockeye salmon, brilliant red.

Then I spot one lone Chinook. She's bigger than the sockeye but almost unnoticeable with her plain brown scales. I feel lucky to see one, because only a few hundred Chinook will make it back to this river this fall.

It has been about four years since the Chinook emerged from an egg, here in this same river. She had to make it downstream as a little fry, alone, and grow big out in the ocean, avoiding the mouths of hungry big fish, seals, sea lions—and Southern Resident orcas.

Chinook salmon. *Seattle Aquarium*

This fall, the Chinook's return journey would have had its own challenges. She had to pass through Seattle's Ballard Locks, a kind of elevator for boats moving between the ocean and the lake. She swam through Lake Washington, dotted with power boats and sailboats, and under highway bridges. Then she reached the Cedar River. It was time to go miles upstream, against the current, through a landscape transformed over decades by roads and railroads, houses and schools, and structures to control floods.

As I watch, the Chinook uses her tail to dig a nest called a redd in the gravelly river bottom, just like her mother did. She'll lay her eggs and die within a week or two, her body perhaps providing food for an eagle as well as nutrients for the nearby trees. The eggs will hatch, and some of those, someday, may grow into mighty fish that a Southern Resident orca like Tahlequah, Shachi, or Oreo can catch to share with her hungry family.

Another Chinook passes by. He was born higher upstream, and he'll keep going until he finds his birthplace, using his sense of smell to remember. After swimming 22 miles away from the ocean, he'll come up against a concrete dam. He'll start searching for a way around it.

More than 100,000 dams have been built on rivers across the United States. Some of them produce hydroelectric power that lets us run our computers, turn on lights, and heat water for our showers. Others divert water to the taps in our homes or to irrigate farms. Still others help control the amount of water going downstream at key times, to prevent flooding. And some dams do all these things.

But when they were built, the dams also did something unintended: they blocked fish from swimming by in either direction. Salmon are born in rivers, and while they grow up out in the ocean, they need to be able to return upstream to lay their eggs. When dams get in the way of migrating salmon, they don't have suitable places to spawn. Salmon numbers drop, and the Southern Resident orcas struggle to find enough to eat.

This Chinook heading up the Cedar River will reach a dam built in 1901. The Cedar River is the main source of drinking water for people who live in Seattle, and the Landsburg Dam diverts water for that purpose. The fish's ancestors would have been stopped there.

But after more than 100 years, in 2003, a fish ladder was added to the dam, so salmon could swim upstream again. Fish ladders are like staircases, where the fish can rest in a pool on each stair before jumping up to the next.

That's good news for this Chinook looking to find a way past the concrete dam. After climbing the fish ladder, he'll be able to access 17 additional miles of river and streams where the water is clean and cool. He'll look for a female and fertilize the eggs she deposits in the gravel.

Scientists count the number of Chinook salmon spawning in the Cedar River by floating in a boat for the entire length and counting every redd. Between 130 and 275 Chinook have been making it past the dam each year for more than a decade now.

This one looks like a fish with a purpose, swimming strong, and I hope he makes it.

~~~~~~~~~

Sometimes salmon get more than a fish ladder. They get a free-flowing river like they had more than a century ago, when Indigenous peoples stewarded the land. More than 1,700 dams were taken out across the country between 1999 and 2019, including more than 100 in the Pacific Northwest. The reasons for dam removal vary: some dams are in bad shape or costly to manage. Sometimes new sources of electricity or drinking water have been developed, so the dams aren't needed anymore. Demolishing a dam can be complicated, expensive, and time-consuming. But in the end, the unstopped river means new hope for salmon and orcas.

These days, there's a spotlight on four dams on the lower Snake River. Located in eastern Washington, they're the heated subject of rallies, newspaper articles, and policy debates.

These four dams are much bigger than the Landsburg Dam, and they have more uses. They produce electricity and provide water for large farms. They also help make the river navigable for barges carrying wheat and other farm products from states like Idaho.

Over the years, fish ladders and other infrastructure have been installed at the lower Snake River dams to help salmon pass over or around them. Those modifications have helped, to some degree. But the salmon are still endangered, and studies show removing the four dams could quadruple the number of adult Chinook returning to the river system.

You'll recall Chinook are exactly the kind of salmon the Southern Resident orcas need because Chinook have the most fat, which translates into energy. A fourfold increase in Chinook from the lower Snake River could be particularly helpful for orcas in K and L pods, like Onyx and Rainshadow. They look for salmon returning to this river system in the springtime. But people have been arguing about whether to remove the dams or leave them in place for years now. People have come to rely on them for water, navigation, and electricity, and find it hard to imagine big changes. Still, conversations are happening about how those services could be replaced, and hopefully the time will come when the dams can be removed to boost the chance of survival for salmon and orcas.

~~~~~~

Farther north in Washington, a story like this has already begun to have a happier ending for salmon. There, the Middle Fork of the Nooksack River is flowing free for the first time in 60 years, after a 25-foot-tall (7.6 m) dam was removed in 2020.

This dam was originally built in 1961 to provide drinking water for a nearby town called Bellingham. Suddenly, Chinook salmon and other fish could no longer swim up to the places where they were born and where baby salmon used to grow big and strong enough to then survive out in the ocean.

Two Tribes, the Nooksack Indian Tribe and the Lummi Nation, approached the City of Bellingham in 2000 hoping to figure out a way to allow salmon to get through. Bellingham agreed to explore alternatives for getting drinking water that wouldn't require keeping the dam. Later, two organizations and a private foundation joined the effort and helped get the money to finalize the plan and put it into action.

Over several months in 2020, that stretch of the river was completely transformed. Workers built a new pipeline to take drinking water to Bellingham, with a screen and smaller pipeline to divert any fish back into the river.

Middle Fork Nooksack Dam, May 2019. *Courtesy of the City of Bellingham*

Site of former Middle Fork Nooksack Dam, April 2021. *Courtesy of the City of Bellingham*

They put up sandbags to divert the water around most of the dam structure, making dry places to work. Then they blasted the dam into pieces.

After cleaning up the pieces and placing boulders in the river channel to return it to a natural state, they removed the sandbags until the river flowed freely over the former dam site. Now, Chinook salmon can once again swim up to spawn in cool waters coming from the mountains.

"That is a very important area up there, culturally, to the Tribe," says Ned Currence, fisheries and resource protection manager for the Nooksack Indian Tribe. "Removing that dam is important to those practices, as is having a free-flowing river and the fish coming with it."

Removal of the dam is expected to boost Chinook salmon populations in the area by at least 30 percent.

"It all comes back to having a healthy Salish Sea again," Tah-Mahs of the Lummi Nation tells me. "It can't be done overnight. We can't change everything that's caused our salmon runs to decline." But removing the Middle Fork Nooksack Dam, she says, is "a step in the right direction."

We need to do more things like this. And we need to speed up the process as much as possible. It took 20 years of planning to remove this dam, and the orcas can't wait another 20 years for new sources of food.

"I just hope we keep taking those steps because there are a lot more steps to accomplish what we need to do," Tah-Mahs says. "If the Salish Sea is healthy and the

Southern Residents once again thrive, we thrive along with them."

~~~~~~~~

As I watch the Chinook and bright-red sockeye salmon swimming up the Cedar River, I find hope in their persistence. They have battled for miles, avoiding barriers and predators, swimming against the current, finally making it to the place where they were born. The eggs they're laying will become a new generation of salmon, supporting Tribal cultures and ceremonies and providing food for the struggling orcas. And all over the Pacific Northwest, members of the human superpod are

A Southern Resident splashes its tail. *Danielle Carter*

working to plant trees along streams, prevent new development in places that would hurt salmon, and remove dams, so salmon and the Southern Resident orcas can recover.

We have no time to waste, but we know what to do. And that's a recipe for hope.

Epilogue:
The Hope in a Superpod, and an Invitation

Every person I talked to has hope the Southern Residents can still recover, and so do I.

We draw hope from many places: The announcement that an orca is pregnant. The birth of a new baby like Tahlequah's Phoenix. The fact that Southern Residents are among the best-studied whales in the world, so we have the information we need to help them. The orcas' intelligence and resilience, and their efforts to adapt to the mess humans have made of their environment. Moments when J, K, and L pod come together in a superpod, filling onlookers with awe.

And finally, there's hope in the superpod of humans working to fix the mess by restoring salmon habitats, cleaning up pollution, quieting the waters, learning more about these orcas, speaking up, and inspiring others.

"Nothing is impossible," says Tah-Mahs of the Lummi Nation.

This human superpod is growing. It has many people besides the ones I've introduced you to in this book. Every year, more jump in to help. For many of them, it's not their job. They simply care too deeply not to act, and they encourage others to do the same.

"Don't underestimate the power of one voice, especially a kid's voice," says scientist Giles.

You are part of this superpod. You can help the orcas or other endangered species in the career you choose as an adult. But you can also help today, wherever you are, whatever your age, and whatever your talents.

"Humans have caused the decline of so many species and are part of the problem for Southern Residents," Marty, the vet who helped treat Scarlet, says. "The cool part is we can also be part of the solution."

Here are some ideas of what you can do now to help the Southern Resident orcas—things that will also help create a healthier environment for other animals and people.

Raise Your Voice

▶ E-mail or call your legislators. Urge them to fund programs to restore salmon habitat, keep toxic chemicals out of the water, and save the orcas. Tell them why you care. Your legislators were elected to represent you, and it's their job to listen. Find their contact information at https://www.usa.gov /elected-officials.

➤ Comment individually or with your class on proposed actions by governments or companies that could help or harm endangered species like the orcas. Those could include potentially harmful proposals like building a new dam, drilling for oil in the ocean, or cutting down trees along a river to make a new parking lot. They could also include helpful actions like removing a dam that's no longer needed, investing in cleaner energy sources, or turning an old industrial site into a park.

➤ Write a letter to your local newspaper with your feelings and thoughts on what needs to happen to protect orcas or other endangered species in your area.

➤ Tell your friends about the Southern Resident orcas.

➤ Make a petition and invite people to sign it, then deliver it to someone who can make bigger changes. When a lot of people ask for the same thing, it can have even more influence on decision-makers.

➤ Follow organizations like Wild Orca (www.wild orca.org) that share urgent policy action ideas on social media.

➤ Check out the latest action ideas at www.seattle aquarium.org/take-action and on my website: www .noranickum.com/orca.

Take Action in Your Community

▶ Do everything you can to mitigate climate change, which is warming rivers and oceans and directly contributing to the decline of salmon. For example, walk or take the bus when that's an option, rather than going by car. Suggest closer-to-home vacations that don't require flying, because airplanes emit even more greenhouse gases per passenger than cars. Put on another sweatshirt instead of turning up the heat. Use reusable water bottles rather than single-use plastic ones.

▶ Keep toxic chemicals out of the water. Talk to your parents about fixing car leaks, not using fertilizers or pesticides on the lawn, and safely disposing of old medicines or chemicals (not putting them down the sink or toilet). It's also important to wash cars at a car-wash instead of in the driveway; in a driveway, any oil, gasoline, soap, and grime will wash into drains that go straight to streams or the ocean rather than first going through a treatment system to remove contaminants.

▶ Consider making a rain garden at your home or school. Rain gardens are bowl-shaped areas with soil and plants that filter pollutants out of the stormwater running off pavement. When the water reaches rivers and the ocean, it'll be clean instead of toxic.

▶ Pick up litter at the beach, along a river, or in your neighborhood—or go bigger and recruit other people to join a cleanup day.

▶ Help plant native trees and other vegetation along rivers and streams. Look up habitat restoration volunteer opportunities online, and you'll find some in your area.

Help the Orcas Forage in Quiet, Safe Waters

▶ Watch endangered orcas from shore. Check out www.thewhaletrail.org for more than 100 recommended sites in California, Oregon, Washington, and British Columbia.

▶ If you go out on a boat with family or friends, be sure to follow the Be Whale Wise speed and distance guidelines at a minimum (www.bewhalewise.org). Stay downwind from whales, if you can, so they don't breathe in the boat's exhaust fumes. Also, remind the captain to turn off the echo sounder if orcas are nearby and it's safe to do so; that way, the pinging sound won't interfere with orcas echolocating to find salmon.

▶ If you're in Washington or British Columbia, report any whale or dolphin sightings to the Whale Report Alert System. That will send warnings to ship captains, so they can slow down and avoid hitting the animals. Download the WhaleReport app to a smartphone or fill out the short form at report.wildwhales .org.

Learn About Indigenous Stewardship

▶ Visit https://sacredsea.org/ to learn more about and support Lummi-led efforts to protect the Salish

Sea, salmon, and Southern Resident orcas and bring Sk'aliCh'elh-tenaut home.

➤ Check out the Native Land Digital map at https:// native-land.ca/ to learn more about the land you live on, including what Indigenous territories have existed and still do exist. There is also a teacher's guide.

Get Creative

➤ Use storytelling, art, photography, or poetry to share the story and beauty of the orcas and inspire others to take action.

➤ When you have a school project, consider focusing it on orca-related issues or other endangered species as an opportunity to learn more and share what you learn with others.

Minimize the Impacts of What You Buy

➤ Choose sustainably harvested salmon and other seafood at grocery stores and restaurants and encourage your family and friends to do the same. This will help ensure there are enough fish left for orcas and other animals to eat. One tool to find out what seafood is sustainable is www.seafoodwatch.org.

➤ Think about where things come from and buy locally made and locally grown products whenever possible. Container ships are a particularly intense source of noise in the orcas' habitat and that of other marine mammals around the world. Those containers are bringing things across the ocean because we're buying them.

▶ Avoid buying things packaged in plastic or taking single-use plastic straws or utensils. Most plastics are made from petroleum, contributing to climate change. In addition, a lot of single-use plastics wind up on beaches and the ocean at the end of their short life; animals can swallow them or get entangled in them.

Help Scientists

▶ Listen to the orcas at orcasound.net and sign up to be a community scientist. Help Orcasound teach its machine to recognize orca calls, so scientists can study them and make new discoveries about orca communication.

▶ Explore community science projects near you at https://scistarter.org/citizen-science. You and your family can collect data, take photos, or make observations that will help scientists learn more about endangered species, monitor changes in the environment, or even make new discoveries.

▶ Symbolically adopt an orca from The Whale Museum or gift one for someone's birthday at www .whalemuseum.org/collections/adopt-an-orca. You'll get to learn more about one of these special animals, and the money will go to programs to protect the orcas. My daughter and I adopted Echo.

Acknowledgments

I'm grateful to everyone who welcomed me aboard boats, into a lighthouse, and on beaches and riverbanks to hear their stories and sometimes catch a glimpse of an orca or a salmon. And, in addition to the experts and advocates who appear in these pages, there are many others who are working hard to help the orcas recover—your dedication gives me hope.

Deep thanks to my agent, Lynnette Novak, and editors Jerome Pohlen and Benjamin Krapohl, who believed in this book and always had clear and reassuring answers to my questions; and to my writing buddies—especially Skylaar Amann, Natasha Zimmers, Carrie Boone, Melissa Lasher, and Kate Allen Fox—for helpful feedback along the way.

Thank you to Danielle Carter and all the other photographers who generously shared incredible images to help bring these words to life, and to Sarah Olson, Chris Erichsen, and Preston Pisellini for the beautiful design work.

My appreciation to Susan, Marc, Penny, Stephanie, Les, Todd, and the rest of the Governor's Orca Task Force team for the opportunity to work with you, and to Dr. Erin Meyer at the Seattle Aquarium for then giving me a job where I can speak up every day for these incredible animals and their ocean home.

A fin-wave to Rachel, Tami, Andrew, Somer, Laura, and so many others—I'm grateful for your encouragement as I wrote this book and all the years of friendship, travels, potlucks, and laughter. I'm so glad to have you in my pod.

Much love and thanks to my great-grandparents, grandparents MacGinitie, and my parents, who made a special place for us on San Juan Island and set a strong example of caring for the environment.

Most of all, gratitude and love to Stuart and Sabina (whose favorite orcas are Echo and Slick). Sabina, I hope, like an orca, you'll always remain close.

J Pod Family Tree

This includes the J pod orcas that are alive at the time of writing, as well as ones that have passed away but are mentioned in this book or help show other family ties. While lines don't connect every orca in J pod, they are all part of one big family with common ancestors. For K and L pod family trees, visit www.noranickum .com/orca.

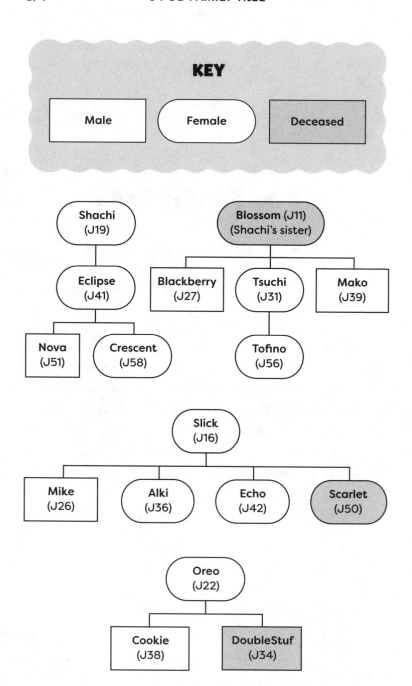

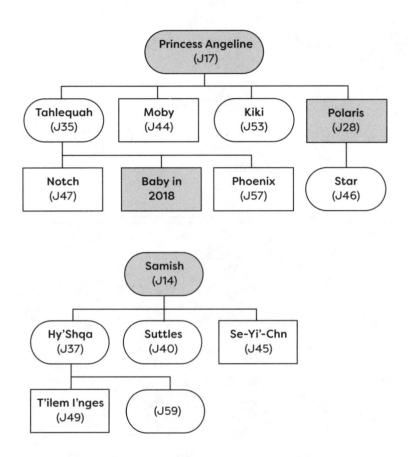

Princess Angeline
(J17)

Tahlequah (J35) • Moby (J44) • Kiki (J53) • Polaris (J28)

Notch (J47) • Baby in 2018 • Phoenix (J57) • Star (J46)

Samish
(J14)

Hy'Shqa (J37) • Suttles (J40) • Se-Yi'-Chn (J45)

T'ilem I'nges (J49) • (J59)

Ruffles
(J1)

Father of Oreo, Blackberry, Mako, Eclipse, and Star, among others

Granny
(J2)

Grandmother of Hy'Shqa, Suttles, and Se-Yi'-Chn

Maps

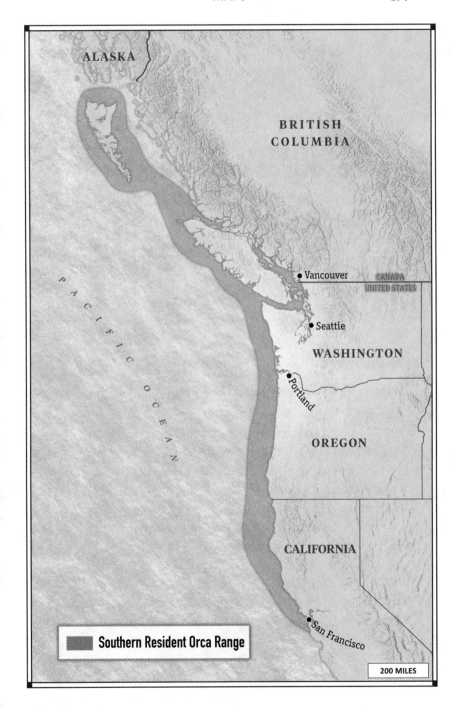

Southern Resident Orca Range

Resources for Readers and Teachers

LEARN MORE

To learn more about organizations mentioned in this book, visit:

Center for Whale Research: www.whaleresearch.com
Orca Network: www.orcanetwork.org
The Sacred Lands Conservancy, a Lummi-led nonprofit: www.sacredsea.org
SeaDoc Society: www.seadocsociety.org
Seattle Aquarium: www.seattleaquarium.org
SeaLife Response + Rehabilitation + and Research (SR3): www.sealifer3.org
Washington State's orca recovery efforts: www.orca.wa.gov
The Whale Museum, Soundwatch, and the orca adoption program: www.whalemuseum.org/collections/meet-the -whales

The Whale Trail's shore-based viewing sites: www.thewhale
   trail.org

Wild Orca: www.wildorca.org

LISTEN AND WATCH

Listen to Southern Resident orca calls: www.orcasound.net

Watch scientists studying orcas: https://videos.fisheries.noaa
   .gov/search?q=southern%20resident

Watch videos from the Lime Kiln Lighthouse webcam:
   www.youtube.com/user/TheWhaleMuseum/videos

FURTHER READING

The following sources may be of particular interest to readers and teachers looking to learn more:

Colby, Jason. *Orca: How We Came to Know and Love the Ocean's
   Greatest Predator.* New York: Oxford University Press, 2018.

Ford, John K. B., Graeme M. Ellis, and Kenneth C. Balcomb.
   Killer Whales: The Natural History and Genealogy of Orcinus
   orca *in British Columbia and Washington.* Second edition.
   UBC Press, Vancouver. Seattle: University of Washington
   Press, 2000.

Gaydos, Joseph K., and Audrey DeLella Benedict. *Explore the
   Salish Sea: A Nature Guide for Kids.* Seattle: Little Bigfoot,
   2018.

Mapes, Lynda. *Orca: Shared Waters, Shared Home.* Seattle:
   Braided River, 2021.

National Oceanic and Atmospheric Administration (NOAA):
   www.fisheries.noaa.gov/west-coast/endangered-species
   -conservation/saving-southern-resident-killer-whales

Perez Valice, Kim. *The Orca Scientists.* New York: Houghton
   Mifflin Harcourt, 2018.

Parry, Rosanne. *A Whale of the Wild*. Illustrated by Lindsay Moore. New York: Greenwillow Books, 2020.

Find more audio and video links, middle school curriculum resources, action ideas, updates on the orcas featured in this book, and a full bibliography on my website: www.noranickum.com/orca.

Notes

1. TAHLEQUAH: 17 DAYS AND 1,000 MILES

"You can imagine her joy": All quotes in this chapter from Jenny Atkinson are from a phone interview with the author, September 24, 2021.

3. THE DAILY SPECIAL

"There hasn't been a generation": All quotes in this chapter from Tah-Mahs are from a video interview with the author, October 12, 2021.

4. CONVERSATIONS BENEATH THE WAVES

"You can interpret it": All quotes in this chapter from Dr. Scott Veirs are from a video interview with the author, September 29, 2021.

"I've seen whales coordinate": All quotes in this chapter from Dr. Michael Weiss are from a video interview with the author, November 7, 2021.

5. THE BONDS OF FAMILY

"They put on a regalia": Tah-Mahs, video interview with the author, October 12, 2021.

"L87's [Onyx] finding": Dr. Michael Weiss, e-mail correspondence with the author, December 6, 2021.

6. DARK HISTORY

"She's just in this teeny tank": All quotes in this chapter from Tah-Mahs are from a video interview with the author, October 12, 2021.

"We saw some whales come": All Ralph Munro quotes in this chapter are from "Meet the Leaders Who Ended Orca Captures in Washington State," filmed December 18, 2018, via Facebook Live, with Lynda Mapes/*Seattle Times*, www.facebook.com/seattletimes/videos/meet-the-leaders-who-ended-orca-captures-in-washington-state/514203989090644/.

"It bothers people": Jason Colby, *Orca: How We Came to Know and Love the Ocean's Greatest Predator*, New York: Oxford University Press, 2018. Citing Commissioner Chairman Victor Scheffer, quoted in Eric Nalder, "US Changes Stand on Whale Captures," Seattle P-I, March 29, 1976.

"I was kind of known": All quotes in this chapter from Taylor Redmond are from a video interview with the author, November 7, 2021.

7. FROM THE AIR

"Helicopter flights are": Aside from the one marked otherwise, all quotes in this chapter from Dr. Holly Fearnbach are from a phone interview with the author, July 20, 2021.

"It's in the middle": NOAA Fisheries & Vancouver Aquarium, "B-Roll: Photogrammetry Research on Southern Resident Killer Whales," https://videos.fisheries.noaa.gov/detail/video/4562510330001/b-roll:-photogrammetry-research-on-southern-resident-killer-whales.

8. WHALE DOCTORS

"It was immediately obvious": All quotes in this chapter from Dr. Marty Haulena are from a phone interview with the author, July 24, 2020.

"That's not the way": All quotes in this chapter from Dr. Joe Gaydos are from a phone interview with the author, July 10, 2020.

"That was our way": Tah-Mahs, video interview with the author, October 12, 2021.

9. MYSTERY OF THE BREACH

"There's an adrenaline rush": All quotes in this chapter from Dr. Bob Otis, Stephanie Dawes, and Kate Laboda are from a group interview conducted by the author in person at the Lime Kiln Lighthouse on July 19, 2021.

"Once they all woke up": Cindy Hansen, video interview with the author, October 18, 2021.

10. WHERE GIANTS CAN STILL DISAPPEAR

"We alert people to": All quotes in this chapter from Cindy Hansen are from a video interview with the author, October 18, 2021.

11. WHY ARE OTHER ORCAS DOING BETTER?

"They can't change": Katharine Gammon, "A Group of Orca Outcasts is Now Dominating an Entire Sea," *Atlantic*, January 29, 2021. Emphases added.

12. THE CANINE IN THE SUPERPOD

"We can't have no *wind"*: All quotes in this chapter from Dr. Deborah Giles are from a phone interview with the author, July 6, 2021.

13. FINDING FRIENDS

"The family structure": All quotes in this chapter from Dr. Michael Weiss are from a video interview with the author, November 7, 2021.

14. AN OCEAN FULL OF NOISE

"It's incredibly challenging": All quotes in this chapter from Dr. Marla Holt are from a video interview with the author, September 17, 2021.

15. QUIETING THE WATERS

"Reducing vessel noise": Author's testimony before the Washington State Senate Agriculture, Water, Natural Resources & Parks Committee, February 12, 2019.

"This is my office": All quotes in this chapter from Taylor Kimball are from a video interview with the author, October 4, 2021.

"We live on this urban fjord": All quotes in this chapter from Donna Sandstrom are from an in-person interview with the author, October 2, 2021.

16. WHEN SALMON RETURN

"That is a very important": Brent Lawrence, "Restoring a River of Life," US Fish and Wildlife Service, accessed December 26, 2021, https://fws.maps.arcgis.com/apps/Cascade /index.html?appid=d3e2066004e74e95bf4b8c4382a51771.

"It all comes back": All quotes in this chapter from Tah-Mahs are from a video interview with the author, October 12, 2021.

EPILOGUE: THE HOPE IN A SUPERPOD, AND AN INVITATION

"Nothing is impossible": Tah-Mahs, video interview with the author, October 12, 2021.

"Don't underestimate the power": Dr. Deborah Giles, phone interview with the author, July 6, 2021.

"Humans have caused": Dr. Marty Haulena, phone interview with the author, July 24, 2020.

Index

Page numbers in *italics* refer to photographs.

action ideas, 164–169
aerial videos and photos, *67*
   drones, 124
   family bonds and, 124–128
   hunting, *124*
   J pod, *126*
   use of, 63–66, 69, 74
age, 39–40
Alki (J36), 68
Alki Beach, 149–151
alpha-numerics, 17
annual census of orcas, 19–20, 58

antibiotics, 76–80
art, 59–60, *59*, 168
Atkinson, Jenny, 10–12, 17

bacterial pneumonia, 76
Bainbridge Island, 98
Balcomb, Ken, 19–20
baleen and baleen whales, 24, 33
Ballard Locks, 154
Be Whale Wise speed and distance guidelines, 167
Bigg, Michael, 16–17, 58, 104–105
Bigg's killer whales. *See* transient orcas
birth, 9

bite marks, 127

Blackberry (J27), 15, *16*, 17, *43*

blowholes, *33*

blubber, 122

boat traffic, 131–133, 139–140, 144–146, 167

boater education, 132–133, 146

breaches and breaching, *3*, *84*, *89*

reasons for, 83–92

Budd Inlet, 56–57, *57*

calls, 30–37

calves
boat traffic and, 140
sharing food with, 26
survival of, 41
Tahlequah's baby, 9–12

Canada, 6, 20, 52–55, 60

captures, 47–58, *48*, *53*, *57*

carcasses, 22

Cedar River, 153–156, 167

census of orcas, 19–20, 58

Center for Whale Research, The, 19, 37–38, 51, 90, 124

Chinook salmon, 23, 153–162, *154*

climate change, 27, 166, 169

Coast Salish Tribes, 28

Columbia River, 94

communication, 30–37, 86

community science, 36–37, 169

Conservation Canines program, 111, 117

container ships, 131, 168

Cookie (J38), 18, 29–30, 89, *89*, *149*

Crescent (J58), 41–42

Currence, Ned, 160

dams, 155–161, *159*

Dawes, Stephanie, 85

DDT, 119, 121

de Silva, Minola Motha, 109, 113, 115, *116*

diet
Chinook salmon, 23
hydration, 27
lack of food, 13, 27
requirements, 23
sharing food, 24–26
Southern Residents, 106–108
studying, 21–23
transient orcas, 106–108

DNA records, 118

dolphins, 24

dorsal fins, 15, 16, *34*, 39, *92*, 105

DoubleStuf (J34), 18, 29–30

drones, 64–66, *65*, 124.
See also aerial videos and photos

Durban, John, 63–71, *65*, 74

Earth Day, 56

Eba (dog), 109–118, *110*, *116*

echolocation, 33, 129–133

Eclipse (J41), *22*, 41–42, *126*, 127

electronic recording tags, 134–139, *134*

Evans, Dan, 56–57

family bonds, 39–45, 123–128

Fearnbach, Holly, 63–71, *65*, 74

ferries, 131, 145

fishermen, 20, 28, *28*

fishing boats, 131

food, 13, 22. *See also* diet

Ford, John, 31, 105

Fraser River, 27, 66

friendship, 123–128

Gaydos, Joe, 74–82

Georgia (K11), 43

Giles, Deborah, 108, 109–121, *113*

Giles, Jim, 112–113

grandmothers, 7–8, 26, 39–42, 45

Granny (J2), 39

Greenpeace, 18, 60

Griffin, Ted, 47–49, 56

Gullickson, Anna, 70

Hansen, Cindy, 89, 97, 99–100

Haulena, Marty, 74–81, *80*

Hays, Michael, 70

health data, 63–71, 119

helicopters, 63–64

Hogan, Jeff, 135

Holt, Marla, 134–140, *137*

how to help the orcas, 164–169

Hugo, 49

humpback whales, 33

hunting, 104–108, *105*, *124*, 125, 139–140

hydration, 27

hydrophones, 29–31, 34–35

Hy'Shqa (J37), 18, 68, 127, *149*

identification of individual orcas, 16–17, 31, 58

Indigenous stewardship, 167–168

J pod

aerial videos and photos, *124*, *126*

Onyx (L87) and, 43

as part of Southern Resident clan, 6

vocalizations of, 31–32

James, Doug, 51

James, Jewell Praying Wolf, 51

K pod

Onyx (L87) and, 43

as part of Southern Resident clan, 6

vocalizations of, 31–32

kelping, 92, *92*
Kenmore Air, 70–71, *70*
kids' observations, 36–37, 88
Kiki (J53), *25*, *44*, 123, *124*, 125
killer whales (term), 4
Kimball, Taylor, 146–148
king salmon. *See* Chinook salmon

L pod
  Onyx (L87) and, 42–43
  as part of Southern Resident clan, 6
  vocalizations of, 31–32
Laboda, Kate, 91
Lake Washington, 154
Landsburg Dam, 155
legislation, 56, 60–61, 106
lifespan, 39–40
Lime Kiln Point State Park, 83–84, *101*
litter, 166
Lolita. *See* Sk'aliCh'elh-tenaut
Lummi (K7), 43
Lummi Nation
  fishing and, 28
  Middle Fork Nooksack Dam and, 158, 160
  orcas and, 42
  Scarlet (J50) and, 77, *78*, 79
  Sk'aliCh'elh-tenaut and, 49–52

Mako (J39), 15, 127
Marine Mammal Commission, 61
Marine Mammal Protection Act (1972), 56, 60, 106
marine parks, 18, 20, 49–58
medicine, 76–80
Mega (L41), 18, *84*, *92*
Miami Seaquarium, 49–52
Middle Fork Nooksack Dam, 158, *159*, 160
Moby (J44), 25, *25*, 44, 127
Monterey Bay, 94
motorboats, 131
Munro, Ralph, 55–57

Native Land Digital, 168
native trees and plants, 167
Nickum, Nora, *144*
Nigel (L95), 95–97
noise, 86, 131, 143, 145, 167
noninvasive research, 111
Nooksack Indian Tribe, 158, 160
Nooksack River, 158
Northern Residents, 26
Northwest Fisheries Science Center, 134
Notch (J47), 9, 18, 25, *25*, 127
Nova (J51), *22*, 41–42, 126–127, *126*

Ocean Sun (L25), 40, 50
Olympia (L32), 42
Onyx (L87), 42–45, *43*, *90*

Orca Network, 51, 89, 97–98, 100–101
orcas
  how to help, 164–169
  name of, 4
  population of, 2, 5–6, 19–20
  speed of, 94
Orcasound, 169
Orcasound network, 29–31, 36
Oreo (J22), 18, 29–30
Otis, Bob, 84, 86–88

Pacific salmon, 23
parasites, 76
PBDEs, 119, 121
PCBs, 119, 121–122
Penn Cove, 47–49, *53*
Phoenix (J57), 14, 25–26, *67*
physical touch, 125–126
pneumonia, 76
pods
  overview, 6
  family bonds and, 42–45, 123–128
  superpods, 4
Point Robinson, *98*, *149*
policy advocacy, 61
pollution, 12–13, 119, 121–122, 166
poop, 22, 110–121, *114*
pregnancy, *67*, 68, 119–120
propellers, 131
Puget Sound, 61

Quiet Sound program, 145

rain gardens, 166
Rainshadow (K37), 136, 138
rake marks, 127
Rappold, Jim, 112–113
Redmond, Taylor, 59–60, *59*
research permits, 23
rest, 86, 87
Rich Passage, 98
rivers
  Cedar River, 153–156, 167
  climate change and, 166
  Columbia River, 94
  dams, 155–161, *159*
  Fraser River, 27
  Nooksack River, 158
  salmon and, 107, 155
  Snake River, 157
Ruffles (J1), 17, 34–35, *34*

saddle-patch patterns, 15, 16, 66
Salish Sea, 1, 6, 28, 30, 36, 52, 96, 105, 131–132, 160–161, 167–168
salmon
  Chinook salmon, 23, 153–162, *154*
  echolocation and, 130
  migration of, 27
  orcas and, 96
  rivers and, 155
  sockeye, 23, 153
  varieties, 23

Samish (J14), 18

Samish Nation, 18

San Juan Island, 1, 27, 34, 47

Sandstrom, Donna,
149–151

satellite tags, 134–139, *134*

Scarlet (J50), *75*, *77*, *78*, *101*
Lummi Nation and, 77,
78, 79
medical intervention for,
71, 73–82

scat, 22, 110–121, *114*

SeaDoc Society, 74

Sealife Response +
Rehabilitation + Research
(SR3), 64

seals and sea lions, *105*,
106–107

seaplanes, 70–71, *70*

Seattle Aquarium, 5, 143

Seattle Marine Aquarium,
52

SeaWorld, 56–57, 78

Shachi (J19), 39–42, *40*, 68

sharing food, 24–26. *See also*
diet

shooting, 20

shore-based whale-watching,
83, 85-86, 149-151, 167

size and health data, 63–71,
93

Sk'aliCh'elh-tenaut, 49–52,
50, *59*

sleep, 86, 87

Snake River, lower, 157

Snake River dams, lower,
157

social bonds, 41–45, 123–128

sonar equipment, 131

soundscape, 30

Soundwatch, *93–94*, 132,
146

Southall Environmental
Associates, Inc, 64

Southern Residents
diet of, 23
how to help, 164–169
identification of, 16
names of, 17–20
population of, 5–6, 19–20
range of, 2, 94
social structure of, 39–45,
123–128
vocalizations of, 31–33, 36

speed, 94

Spieden (J8), 43

Spirit (L22), 18

spyhops, 90, *90*

Star (J46), 123

stress levels, 119

Stuart Island, 38

superpods, 4, 7, 47

Surprise! (L86), *132*, *134*

Suttles (J40), 123

swim bladders, 130

Tahlequah (J35), *13*, *25*
baby of, 9–14
family bonds and, 23–25
pregnancy of, *67*

Tah-Mahs, *28*
  on fishing, 28
  on the Middle Fork
    Nooksack Dam, 160
  on orcas, 42, 164
  Scarlet (J50) and, 79
  on Sk'aliCh'elh-tenaut,
    49–52
tail-slaps, 86, *161*
taking action, 164–169
teeth, 24
temporary tags, 134–139, *134*
threats
  boat traffic, 131–133,
    139–140
  captures, 47–58, *48*, *53*
  lack of food, 13, 27
  noise, 86, 131, 143, 145, 167
  pollution, 12–13, 120–122
T'ilem I'nges (J49), 126–127,
  126
Tofino (J56), 123, *124*, 125
Tokitae. *See*
  Sk'aliCh'elh-tenaut
toothed whales, 24
toxic chemicals, 12–13, 119,
  121–122, 166
tracking tags, 95–97, 134–
  139, *134*

transient orcas, 104–108,
  105, *114*
Tsuchi (J31), 15, *16*

underwater microphones,
  29–31, 34–35

Vancouver Aquarium, 74
Veirs, Scott, 29–30, *32*, 35–37
vocalizations, 30–37

Washington State
  Legislature, 143–144, *144*
Wasser, Sam, 111
weight data, 68–69
Weiss, Michael, 37–38, 44,
  124–127
Whale Museum, 10–11,
  37–38, 93, 132, 169
Whale Report Alert System,
  167
Whale Trail, The, 149–151,
  167
whale-watching industry,
  132–133, 144
Whidbey Island, 47
Wild Orca, 108, 165
Wild Orca Seaplane, 70–71,
  70